**At Issue**

# Is Foreign Aid Necessary?

# Other Books in the At Issue Series:

## At Issue

# I Is Foreign Aid Necessary?

*David Haugen and Susan Musser, Book Editors*

**GREENHAVEN PRESS**
*A part of Gale, Cengage Learning*

**GALE**
CENGAGE Learning·

Detroit • New York • San Francisco • New Haven, Conn • Waterville, Maine • London

Elizabeth Des Chenes, *Director, Publishing Solutions*

© 2013 Greenhaven Press, a part of Gale, Cengage Learning.

Gale and Greenhaven Press are registered trademarks used herein under license.

*For more information, contact:*
Greenhaven Press
27500 Drake Rd.
Farmington Hills, MI 48331-3535
Or you can visit our Internet site at gale.cengage.com

For product information and technology assistance, contact us at

Gale Customer Support, 1-800-877-4253
For permission to use material from this text or product, submit all requests online at www.cengage.com/permissions

Further permissions questions can be e-mailed to permissionrequest@cengage.com

Articles in Greenhaven Press anthologies are often edited for length to meet page requirements. In addition, original titles of these works are changed to clearly present the main thesis and to explicitly indicate the author's opinion. Every effort is made to ensure that Greenhaven Press accurately reflects the original intent of the authors. Every effort has been made to trace the owners of copyrighted material.

Cover image © Images.com/Corbis.

**LIBRARY OF CONGRESS CATALOGING-IN-PUBLICATION DATA**

Is foreign aid necessary? / David Haugen and Susan Musser, book editors.
    p. cm. -- (At issue)
    Includes bibliographical references and index.
    ISBN 978-0-7377-6187-0 (hardcover) -- ISBN 978-0-7377-6188-7 (pbk.)
    1. Economic assistance, American--Government policy. I. Haugen, David M., 1969- II. Musser, Susan.
    HC60.I74 2012
    338.91'73--dc23
                                                              2012025800

Printed in the United States of America
1 2 3 4 5 6 7 16 15 14 13 12

# Contents

# Introduction

For roughly a century, the United States has channeled a portion of its public funds into foreign assistance. Given in the form of military weaponry, food, medicines, money, and other types of support, US foreign aid currently reaches over 180 countries around the world. The motivations for such largesse are diverse: Congress has authorized aid to stabilize foreign governments, acquire strategic allies, help victims of poverty and disaster, encourage economic development, and develop international trade. In 1961, President John F. Kennedy inaugurated the United States Agency for International Development (USAID), a federal agency that oversees a large part of the humanitarian and long-term development assistance (provided chiefly through loans and grants) doled out to nations in need. However, USAID is only one part of a large aid network that includes loans, donations, and other assistance from the State Department and the US Department of Agriculture, as well as various nongovernmental organizations (NGOs), churches, and private charities.

America's spirit of giving, however, has never escaped criticism. Several modern historians argue that the rebuilding of Europe after World War II clearly had the objective of keeping communism from gaining control of key Western governments. Throughout the ensuing Cold War, foreign aid was viewed as a means of propping up "friendly" governments in Asia, Africa, and Latin America that seemed beset by popular uprisings that threatened to spread socialism in these regions. In addition to purporting hidden political agendas on the part of the US government, critics have charged recipient governments with misusing or redirecting aid, often indicting foreign administrations for using aid money to enrich an elite few instead of dispensing it to their truly needy citizens. In 1962, George Champion, chairman of Chase Manhattan Bank, delivered a speech to the New York Chamber of Commerce in which he argued that America's foreign aid needed an overhaul because the programs were failing to make a difference in developing nations. Champion charged: "Quite often enterprise and investment within these countries is frustrated or misdirected by a maze of government controls, inflation, or even low standards of civic rectitude. And yet I firmly believe that the manner in which foreign aid has been handled very often encourages and supports such undesirable internal developments." Champion proposed the creation of a large, multinational aid organization that would coordinate all aid efforts and promote free enterprise in recipient countries, but even if his vision never came to be, others echoed his warning that too much assistance was being wasted on those governments with "low standards of civic rectitude."

In 2004, responding to growing concern over financing corrupt governments, President George W. Bush created the Millennium Challenge Corporation (MCC), a new federal agency that would disperse a designated amount of foreign assistance (apart from USAID) through a competitive process in which needy countries vied for funds based on their allegiance to the principles of good governance. That is, a recipient nation must demonstrate a need, offer a strategy for wisely using aid monies, and show a commitment to free markets and the rule of law. In a May 12, 2005 speech, the first CEO of the Millennium Challenge Corporation, Paul Applegarth, told conference attendees at Northwestern University: "Economic growth is sustainable in countries that adopt and maintain policies that support it. Countries that are actively fighting corruption, that are providing an environment for a free and open exchange of ideas that will help identify and overcome obstacles to growth, that are investing in health and education, and that are creating an enabling environment for businesses to grow, are putting themselves on the fastest track to poverty reduction and growth." Seventeen countries acquired compacts with the MCC in the first year of operation, and Bush promised that aid funds within the Millennium Challenge Account would steadily increase as the program proved its merits. The MCC has made good on that promise, and over time more countries have earned compacts. The program does have its critics, most of whom object that foreign aid should not come with strings attached and that refraining from releasing funds to less-than-perfect governments punishes the people who suffer under those governments and who may need help. Advocates, however, point out that only MCC funds are withheld and that other US aid assistance is still available to most countries.

The administration of President Barack Obama has kept the MCC afloat and in 2012 put forth a 2013 budget that earmarks $51.6 billion dollars for the US State Department and other foreign aid demands. Obama's implementation strategy is based on his conviction that aid goals need to be reformed. In a September 22, 2010 speech outlining his policy directive for foreign aid, Obama said: "Instead of just managing poverty, we have to offer nations and peoples a path out of poverty." Thus, the US and its partners must, in Obama's view, offer long-term economic assistance that gets results in putting foreign markets on their feet. "The purpose of development— and what's needed most right now—is creating the conditions where assistance is no longer needed," the president remarked. "So we will seek partners who want to build their own capacity to provide for their people. We will seek development that is sustainable." Building on the MCC model but dropping the explicit constraint of "good governance," Obama pledged continued US support to countries that show a "commitment to development."

Current opposition to Obama's plans and budgetary requirements argue that the United States is still too often handing over taxpayer money to countries that show little governmental reform and seem to perpetually struggle with creating viable markets. In a January 2, 2012 editorial for the Save America Foundation, Fred Brownbill writes, "Many governments steal the foreign aid money that the US sends to help the poor. Food aid, too, is frequently stolen. The money simply isn't getting where it needs to go. But worse yet, when the food and money does go where it needs to go, many times it does not help." One of the most vocal critics of US foreign aid policy is Senator Rand Paul, a Republican from Kentucky. Paul has told news sources that welfare to foreign governments does not help and that, in the depressed global economy that resulted from failing markets in 2008, America should find uses for taxpayer money at home. In a January 26, 2011 interview on CNN, Paul stated that a majority of Americans agreed with him that "when we're short of money, where we can't do the things we need to do in our country, we certainly shouldn't be shipping the money overseas."

*At Issue: Is Foreign Aid Necessary?* collects a host of political and economic commentators who present their views on the state of US foreign aid in the new millennium. Some question whether aid is delivering on its promises, while others offer ways in which the various types of aid programs could be reformed to produce better results. Although all the assembled critics recognize that developing countries still suffer from poverty and problematic health issues in the twenty-first century, not everyone agrees that American aid can solve these social ills. Some believe it is a national duty to help the poor; others advocate that charity begins at home. Reconciling these divergent views may define exactly how the country proceeds in distributing America's vast wealth.

# 1

# Foreign Aid Helps Recipient Nations Escape Poverty

*Jeffrey D. Sachs*

*Jeffrey D. Sachs is a professor of economics at Columbia University. He is also the founder and co-president of the Millennium Promise Alliance, an organization working to end global poverty and hunger. Sachs has authored several works on addressing economic equality, including* The End of Poverty: Economic Possibilities for Our Time.

*Though skeptics seem bent on convincing donor nations that the developing world abuses foreign aid, the truth is that health and economic assistance are improving the lives of people in poor countries. Providing food, healthcare, and technology and infrastructure improvements has benefited many communities in the poorest parts of Africa, for example, leading locals to build upon those successes. It is the duty of the developed world to ignore the naysayers and lend a helping hand that can save lives and eliminate the direst forms of poverty around the globe.*

The developing world often seems like highway traffic. Countries such as China, India, and Chile are in a slipstream of rapid economic growth, closing the technological gap with the industrialized countries, while nations such as Nepal, Niger, and Sudan are rushing in the reverse direction, with rising unrest, confrontation, drought, and disease.

The costs of the economic failures are enormous for the whole world because conflicts, terrorism, the drug trade, and refugees spill across national borders.

*We can help ensure the successful economic development of the poorest countries. We can help them escape from poverty.*

But drivers can change direction, and so can countries. India, China, and Chile were hardly success stories in the 1960s and 1970s. All were in turmoil, beset by poverty, hunger, and political instability. Their economic transformations show that today's "basket cases" can be tomorrow's emerging markets.

Those who contend that foreign aid does not work—and cannot work—are mistaken. These skeptics make a career of promoting pessimism by pointing to the many undoubted failures of past aid efforts. But the fact remains that we can help ensure the successful economic development of the poorest countries. We can help them escape from poverty. It's in our national interest to do so.

## Three Steps out of Poverty

The first step out of rural poverty almost always involves a boost in food production to end cycles of famine. Asia's ascent from poverty in the last 40 years began with a "green revolution." Food yields doubled or tripled. The Rockefeller Foundation helped with the development and propagation of high-yield seeds, and US aid enabled India and other countries to provide subsidized fertilizer and seeds to impoverished farmers. Once farmers could earn an income, they could move on to small-business development.

A second step out of poverty is an improvement in health conditions, led by improved nutrition, cleaner drinking water, and more basic health services. In the Asian success stories, child mortality dropped sharply, which, in turn, led to smaller families because poor parents gained confidence that their children would survive to adulthood.

The third step is the move from economic isolation to international trade. Chile, for instance, has become the chief source of off-season fruit in the US during the past 20 years by creating highly efficient supply chains. China and India have boomed as exporters of manufacturing goods and services, respectively. In all three, trade linkages were a matter of improved connectivity—roads, power, telecommunications, the Internet, and transport containerization.

## Many Developing Nations Are Showing Progress

Today, the skeptics like to claim that Africa is too far behind, too corrupt, to become a China or India. They are mistaken. An African green revolution, health revolution, and connectivity revolution are all within reach. Engineers and scientists have already developed the needed tools. [Focusing on helping villages meet development goals] the Millennium Villages project, which I and a group of colleagues developed, is now rapidly expanding in 10 countries in Africa and is showing that this triple transformation—in improved agriculture, health, and connectivity—is feasible.

Improved seed varieties, fertilizers, irrigation, and trucks have all helped convert famine into bumper crops in just one or two productive growing seasons.

*In any part of the world, the poorest of the poor want a chance for a better future, especially for their children. Give them the tools, and they will grasp the chance.*

Malaria is under control. Farmers have access to capital to make the change from subsistence to cash crops. Children are being treated for worms and receive a midday meal to help keep them healthy and in school.

Skeptics said that African peasants would not grow more food, that fertilizers would go missing, that bed nets would be cut up to make wedding veils, and that local officials would block progress.

The truth is the opposite. In any part of the world, the poorest of the poor want a chance for a better future, especially for their children. Give them the tools, and they will grasp the chance.

Aid skeptics such as professor William Easterly, author of the recent book "The White Man's Burden." are legion. Instead of pointing to failures, we need to amplify the successes—including the green revolution, the global eradication of smallpox, the spread of literacy, and, now, the promise of the Millennium Villages.

## Targeted Aid to Specific Community Needs

The standards for successful aid are clear. They should be targeted, specific, measurable, accountable, and scalable. They should support the triple transformation in agriculture, health, and infrastructure. We should provide direct assistance to villages in ways that can be measured and monitored.

The Millennium Villages project relies on community participation and accountability to ensure that fertilizers, medicines, and the like are properly used.

Millennium Promise, an organization I cofounded, champions and furthers the development of the Millennium Villages project. It has partnered with the Red Cross, UNICEF, the UN Foundation, Centers for Disease Control, and the World Health Organization to get antimalaria bed nets to the children of Africa.

In this fragile and conflict-laden world, we must value life everywhere by stopping needless disease and deaths, promoting economic growth, and helping ensure that our children's lives will be treasured in the years ahead.

# 2

# Foreign Aid Benefits US National Security

*Rajiv Shah*

*Since December 2009, Rajiv Shah has served as the administrator of the United States Agency for International Development. He formerly presided as under secretary for research, education, and economics and as chief scientist at the US Department of Agriculture.*

*The United States Agency for International Development (USAID) is the chief national distributor of global aid. USAID is working to provide economic, health, and other aid services to developing nations across the globe in order to raise standards of living and to save lives mired in severe poverty. In addition to these worthy aims, USAID projects spread American values and promote democracy in recipient lands. Such ambassadorship helps stabilize nations torn by war and civil unrest, thus benefiting US national security by quelling conflict and showing the world's disaffected that America is dedicated to improving their lives. Foreign aid is one of the best and cheapest tools the United States has to prevent violence and instill in recipients the desire to embrace democratic principles and focus their energies on economic success.*

The developing world looms large in America's economic fortunes. Our country's fastest-growing markets, representing roughly half of U.S. exports, are developing countries.

Rajiv Shah, "United States Agency for International Development: The Modern Development Enterprise," speech given at the Center for Global Development, January 19, 2011. www.usaid.gov.

In 2009, we exported over half a trillion dollars to those countries and more than 90 percent of those export revenues went to small and medium-sized U.S. companies—precisely those firms that are the engines of job growth in our country. That's why for every 10 percent increase we see in exports, there's a 7 percent decrease in the unemployment rate here at home.

But in addition to keeping us competitive in tomorrow's global economy, our assistance keeps us safe today. In the most volatile regions of Afghanistan and Pakistan, we work side-by-side with the military, playing a critical role in our nation's efforts to stabilize countries and build responsive, viable local governance. On a daily basis, our people put themselves in harm's way, and they suffer casualties, working on the same problems as our military while using far different tools.

## Stabilizing Afghanistan and Pakistan

In Afghanistan, we're helping to improve agricultural yields in the Argandab Valley, stabilizing a region in which hour military suffered casualties to secure. As a result, farmers shipped the first agricultural exports out of Kandahar export in 40 years. We've also rebuilt the civil service in the southeast and helped fuel a 40 percent reduction in the growth of opium poppies that fund Taliban [the former, oppressive religious regime that ruled Afghanistan] operations.

> *I can tell you, whether it's establishing basic health services for Afghans or whether it's creating local shuras in northwest Pakistan to promote viable sub-national governance, USAID's work is absolutely critical to keeping us safe and secure.*

In Pakistan, our foreign service national workforce and our support for local organizations allow us to go where others often cannot. Through our office of transition initiatives alone, we now administer nearly 1400 small-scale development projects in the Federally Administered Tribal Areas of Pakistan, responding quickly to local needs.

In the Malakand province, we renovated 150 schools so that children seeking an education can look behind extremist madrassas and find viable alternatives. I visited both countries multiple times over the last year, and I can tell you, whether it's establishing basic health services for Afghans or whether it's creating local shuras in northwest Pakistan to promote viable sub-national governance, USAID's work is absolutely critical to keeping us safe and secure.

As a community, we must strengthen the role we play in these situations. Based on decades of experience working in conflict environments, next month [February 2011] we will unveil USAID's first-ever policy on the role of development assistance in countering violent extremism and counterinsurgency.

Our policy will build on tools like the District Stabilization Framework, which was built in close collaboration with the Pentagon to bring a more data-oriented approach to identifying the true drivers or local instability and resolving them with more effect. Ultimately, our work needs to increase short-term stability while easing the transition between conflict, fragile peace and long-term development.

---

*Development is a lot cheaper than sending soldiers.*

---

## Preventing Violence and Promoting Democracy

But when it comes to national security, our work goes far beyond partnering with the military to combat [the terrorist organization] al-Qaida and the Taliban. Over the last several decades, USAID, in partnership with the Colombia government, has launched several successful programs aimed at directing farmers away from coca cultivation. We've seen cultivation plummet by as much as 85 percent since 2005 in areas of that country where we did in fact do our work.

And while USAID can work in active conflict or help countries transition away from violence, the most important thing we can do is prevent violence in the first place. As Secretary [of Defense Robert] Gates himself has said, development is a lot cheaper than sending soldiers. He's also said that everyone should invest more in USAID.

In Southern Sudan, the USAID mission is working hard to ensure that inspiring expression of democracy does not lead to yet another bout of regional bloodshed. Our team has been in Juba for years, implementing projects that set the stage for the recent, historic referendum. In fact, many other bilateral and multilateral partners like DFID [Britain's Department for International Development] and the World Bank co-invest in programs and projects we've helped set up in that part of Sudan.

---

*When we prevent violence in Southern Sudan, we are not just avoiding future military involvement. We're also expressing American values.*

---

Five months ago, when the world seemed convinced that the recently completed referendum would not occur, our team worked with the Southern Sudan Referendum Commission, the United Nations and local NGOs [nongovernmental organizations] to design, procure and pre-position ballots. We believed in being prepared. That foresight allowed the historic referendum to proceed on schedule and in an orderly manner. So far, as we all know, the region has avoided a descent into large-scale violence, and we keep our fingers crossed for a positive and effective outcome.

## Spreading American Values

Having lived through genocides in Rwanda and Darfur [in Sudan], we remain committed to preventing the kind of ethnic persecution we've so often seen in that region in the past. When we prevent violence in Southern Sudan, we are not just avoiding future military involvement. We're also expressing American values.

When school children organize bake sales to pay for antimalarial bed nets, it sounds like they're health economists because they know the efficiency of that intervention, but they are expressing American values. When more American families give money to the relief effort in Haiti than watch the Super Bowl, that is an expression of American values. When church groups across the United States raise money and volunteer to support children who are orphaned by AIDS in sub-Saharan Africa, they are expressing American values.

*Faith-based organizations not only express the moral values of millions of Americans. They also provide some of the most dependable support systems for millions of people in the developing world.*

Just last week, I attended a mass commemorating the one-year anniversary of the tragic earthquake in Haiti. I was impressed on the way out by a flier Catholic Relief Services [CRS] distributed describing all of the great work they were doing to protect survivors and save lives in Port au Prince [Haiti's capital].

## Working with Experienced Faith-Based Organizations

I'm proud to know that USAID is one of CRS's largest supporters, but I'm also proud to know that we support a wide range of faith-based organizations from Samaritans First to the American Jewish World Service. Faith-based organizations not only express the moral values of millions of Americans. They also provide some of the most dependable support systems for millions of people in the developing world. In Kenya, for example, 30 percent of all health-care services are provided by Christian hospitals.

Our success depends on listening to these groups actively, connecting with them deeply, leveraging the trust and the partnership they've nurtured in communities where they've practiced for a very long time and supporting the vital work of organizations of faith around the world.

I know that my remarks today [January 19, 2011] reflect a lot of tough calls for change. I know that over the last year and in the coming year, I've called for a lot of shifts in how our community and how our agency and how our staff operate. Change is never easy, and I thank you all for the difficult choices you've made to usher in a new way of doing business in global development.

## A Duty and a Responsibility to Aid the Poor

But I've asked for this change because I believe it is critical to achieving the peace, prosperity and security we all seek. I believe what leading CEOs like Indra K. Nooyi of Pepsi Co. and A.G. Lafley of Proctor & Gamble believe: that the future of American prosperity will reside on progress in the developing world.

I believe what military leaders like General David Petraeus and Admiral Mike Mullen believe: that development is critical to keeping America safe and secure and keeping American soldiers out of harm's way. I believe what religious leaders like Pastor Rick Warren [of Saddleback Church] and Bishop Charles Blake [of the Church of God in Christ] believe: that as beneficiaries of peace and progress, we have a moral obligation and responsibility to assist those less fortunate.

And I believe what political leaders like [former Republican US Senator from Tennessee] Bill Frist and [former Democratic US Senator from South Dakota] Tom Daschle believe: that promoting international development is not a Democratic value or a Republican value. It is an American value, and it serves American interests.

But I really believe what President Obama and Secretary Clinton believe that together, we have the power to create the world we seek if we have the courage to embrace the opportunity and the willingness to do things differently.

Now is the time to invest in USAID's capabilities so we see the day when our assistance is no longer needed.

# 3

# Foreign Aid Has Been a Failure

*Andrei Schleifer*

*Born in Russia, Andrei Schleifer serves as professor of economics at Harvard University. He has worked in establishing free market institutions in a number of countries, including Russia. Schleifer is the author of several books, including* Privatizing Russia *and* The Grabbing Hand: Government Pathologies and their Cures. *He is the winner of the 1999 John Bates Clark Medal, given to a top American economist under 40.*

*The late economist Peter Bauer was correct in his belief that foreign aid is a failure. According to Bauer, countries advance economically by protecting individual enterprise and limiting the role of government. Most foreign aid never reaches needy recipients but rather finances and preserves the control of governments and bureaucrats over private individuals and their economic lives. Donor governments likewise pursue their own objectives, often distinct from economic and social development of recipient nations, in disbursing aid. For these reasons, foreign aid, at least as currently practiced, has done little to improve the economic lives of the poor.*

Peter Bauer was one of the greatest development economists in history. He was an advocate of property rights protection and free trade before these ideas became commonplace. He appreciated before others did the crucial roles of en-

Andrei Schleifer, "Peter Bauer and the Failure of Foreign Aid," *Cato Journal*, Fall 2009, pp. 379–90. Copyright © 2009 by the Cato Institute. All rights reserved. Reproduced by permission.

trepreneurship and trade in development. He was also one of thee earliest opponents of the overpopulation thesis, recognizing that the poor like the rich should have the right to choose the number of children they have, that many developing countries are underpopulated, and that population growth will anyhow slow down once they become richer. Bauer's writings are remarkable for their deep humanity and commitment to the welfare of the people in the developing world, but without the fake sanctimony that characterizes much of the modern rhetoric.

## Bauer's Criticism of the Aid Model

Bauer is perhaps best known as a persistent and articulate critic of foreign aid. At least since 1972, he saw it as not only failing to speed up, but actually hurting economic development. He started his criticism when foreign aid to the developing world was only getting underway, and never wavered. He defined foreign aid as "a transfer of resources from the *taxpayer* of a donor country to the *government* of a recipient country." Needless to say, this did not endear him to the aid establishment. . . .

---

*Aid destroys economic incentives, leads to misallocation of scarce resources, and so not only fails to jump start, but actually undermines growth.*

---

Bauer and subsequent writers have advanced several reasons for this dismal performance of foreign aid. The ostensible purpose of aid, at least in the post—World War II era, was to stimulate economic growth. The intellectual support for many of the policy recommendations for how to allocate aid in order to stimulate economic growth was based on the big push model. According to that model, what keeps countries behind is insufficient investment across sectors of the economy and in infrastracture. To the extent that foreign aid supplies investment capital, it jump starts economic growth, and initiates a virtuous cycle whereby investment generates income and thus raises the economic return to further investment.

Bauer relentlessly criticized the big push model. He argued that foreign aid providers do not know which investments are appropriate for a developing economy, so aid money is poured into bad projects (also known as white elephants), which not only fail to encourage economic growth, but divert scarce human and other resources away from productive uses. The limited institutional and human capabilities of a country are wasted on unproductive rather than productive activities. Aid destroys economic incentives, leads to misallocation of scarce resources, and so not only fails to jump start, but actually undermines growth. . . .

---

*The role of kickbacks, bribes, and campaign contributions in shaping decisions on foreign aid by donor countries is only beginning to be understood.*

---

## Aid Money Is Sidetracked to Various Political Interests

One approach is to follow the long and intricate road that a dollar of a Western taxpayers money must follow before it reaches a needing recipient in a developing country. Think about what happens to that dollar. First, it must be allocated by the donor country's government. That government has its national political, military, and economic objectives, such as supporting friendly states, selling its food and weapons, promoting its own consultants, intervening in international conflicts, and so on. Traditionally, much of bilateral foreign aid has been tied to purchases from donor countries, although apparently this phenomenon has seen some decline. Many of these objectives have little to do with development. A large chunk of the U.S. development assistance, for example, is military support for Egypt and Israel.

Even for the part of the Western taxpayers dollar intended for development, the donor country's government can have incorrect or even bizarre ideas for how to spend it. Think of the Swedish government's support of socialist policies in Tanzania, which most observers believe have failed. Or the French governments support of petty Francophile dictators in its ex-colonies in West Africa, designed to expand the French sphere of influence. In a similar vein, countries may choose to spend "development" money on their own firms and contractors undertaking projects abroad. Much of the money, of course, stays at home. The role of kickbacks, bribes, and campaign contributions in shaping decisions on foreign aid by *donor* countries is only beginning to be understood.

---

*Many a developing country leader has become a billion-aire courtesy of foreign aid.*

---

But suppose that some fraction of that initial dollar actually reaches a bilateral or multilateral development agency with the intention that it be spent on actual development as opposed to arms procurement or transfers to Western firms and farms. In addition to having significant staffs of their own, these institutions often have ideas of their own, as well as constraints on how to spend the money dictated by donor priorities. For example, coordinated investment spending à la big push was the prevailing development wisdom for much of the 1970s, which may have resulted in a significant misallocation of resources. Furthermore, development institutions have a strong incentive to spend—push the money out (this is the true push). This means that countries willing to accept the most money, as grants or as loans, and to spend it on the biggest projects, become the most attractive candidates for aid. There is not much evidence that aid is allocated to countries that spend it more wisely.

## Corruption and Theft of Aid Money

But let us keep following whatever is left of the Western taxpayer's dollar. Suppose that some fraction of that original dollar is now lent or given as a grant to a government in a developing country for some purpose that may contribute to development. As has been extensively documented, in many instances the first instinct of the officials receiving the funds is to steal them. Many a developing country leader has become a billionaire courtesy of foreign aid. When the money is not stolen by the leader, there are the various ministers, officials, and other bureaucrats who all want a cut.

This problem is particularly severe in the case of foreign loans, which is how the World Bank and the International Monetary Fund [IMF] deliver most foreign aid. Because loans are sovereign obligations of the receiving country, it is difficult for the donors to control how they are spent: conditionality is typically a failure. Because loans come in the form of cash, they are particularly vulnerable to diversion. And of course, unlike aid grants, loans become the obligation of the borrowing country, and therefore are supposed to be eventually repaid—a tax on future resources.

The consequences of this structure have been dramatic. The loans to developing countries have come to be known as "odious debt" because the proceeds are stolen by the governments and the citizens are taxed to repay. The debt has been largely rescheduled and rarely repaid. Indeed, donor countries came under severe criticism for even asking for repayment. In many countries, especially in Latin America, borrowing from the IMF and the World Bank was condemned by the left as the attempt by the capitalist West to destabilize developing economies. Far from being seen as an exercise in benevolence that promoted development, foreign aid in the form of loans energized the left in its support of economic and social policies most antithetical to development.

The diversion of foreign aid by officials in recipient countries is not, unfortunately, just a lump sum tax. To begin, when diversion of aid money is a significant issue, recipient governments begin to seek assistance for projects from which it is easier to steal and where spending is harder to monitor. The composition of aid spending is then distorted. And just as donor countries want to allocate aid money for national priorities, recipient governments want to spend it for their national priorities that may, but need not, coincide with development needs. The recipient governments want to allocate money to their friends, families, and political supporters, to pursue military and foreign policy goals, etc. Like the donor governments, the recipient governments often, perhaps even more often, have bizarre ideas about development. And so another fraction of that Western taxpayer's dollar is wasted.

> *The lesson of development economics of the last decade is that there is tremendous corruption, waste, and resource misallocation at every stage.*

But remember that money, or what is left of it, is still in the recipient country's capital. The small piece of it designated for some activity that resembles economic or social development is yet to be spent for that purpose. That piece still needs to pass through the treasury, the spending ministry, the regional offices, and the actual spenders in the developing country. At each turn, some fraction is diverted, misspent, or wasted. According to [World Bank economist Ritva] Reinikka and [Stockholm University economist Jakob] Svensson, 13 cents out of each dollar of the Ugandan government's expenditure on schools actually reached those schools. Not all of that waste is malevolent. Western governments have a lot of trouble spending money efficiently; the human and administrative capabilities of developing country governments are considerably lower, as is the efficiency of their spending.

## Unwise Spending by Recipients

Last but not least, when the money reaches a designated recipient—a bridge builder, a teacher, or a farmer—that recipient must spend it wisely. The bridge builder must build the bridge; the teacher must show up at school; the fanner must use his fertilizer. None of these can be taken for granted. Indeed, the lesson of development economics of the last decade is that there is tremendous corruption, waste, and resource misallocation at every stage. Bridges are not built (or collapse soon after if built); teachers stay at home; and farmers retain old production techniques.

> *Pro-market economic policies have been as important as anything we know of in fostering economic development. Yet foreign aid, by relaxing the budget constraint of the government, in many instances has the effect of delaying the introduction of such good policies.*

The bottom line is that perhaps a few pennies of the original Western taxpayers dollar are actually spent as might be designed and implemented by a benevolent and effective social planner. The rest is wasted or diverted. [Professor of Economics at New York University William] Easterly suggests that a trillion dollars has been spent on foreign aid since World War II. But how much has actually been delivered wisely to the intended recipients of that aid? Viewed from the perspective of a dollar traveling from the Western taxpayer's pocket to the intended ultimate recipient, the failure of foreign aid is not all that puzzling.

## The Failure of Accountability

As important, the diversion of most of the dollar before a few pennies reach an intended recipient is not development neutral—this diversion may actually undermine development because it interferes with the political and institutional processes that might actually be beneficial to a country. For example, many social scientists believe in the idea going back to the Magna Carta, and which has some empirical support as well, that governments should have to raise taxes to finance their spending, so that they are forced to seek the consent of the governed. By breaking the link between government resources and its ability to tax, foreign aid might undermine the basic contract between the government and the governed. And to the extent that the evolution of indigenous political institutions is a central element of economic and social development, these adverse effects of foreign aid might be as significant as the meager benefits it provides.

Another way to make this point is to focus on economic policy. Pro-market economic policies have been as important as anything we know of in fostering economic development. Yet foreign aid, by relaxing the budget constraint of the government, in many instances has the effect of delaying the introduction of such good policies. In the 1980s and 1990s, the donors tried to address this problem by linking aid to policy reform. The donors often failed, because the client governments resisted, because they failed to deliver policy reform even when they accepted conditionality, and because conditionality was severely criticized in the West for interfering with the sovereignty of developing countries. Today, the promotion of good policies through conditionality is at best a half-hearted foreign aid priority.

The bottom line is that Bauer was correct about foreign aid. Foreign aid has failed to meet its principal objective: to spur economic growth. The reasons for its failure are probably multiple and more complex—and more numerous—than just a failed model of development. But the evidence has broadly corroborated Bauer's view: an important instance of economic analysis making a correct prediction about reality in advance.

# 4

# Congress Should Cut Foreign Aid

*Dick Morris*

*Dick Morris is a political writer and commentator who worked as an advisor to former President Bill Clinton when he was governor of Arkansas. He wrote* Behind the Oval Office: Winning the Presidency in the Nineties *as an inside look at Clinton's run for presidency. His most recent book,* Revolt! How to Defeat Obama and Repeal His Socialist Programs, *was released in 2011.*

*In the midst of a crisis that threatens to shut down the US government unless Congress can significantly cut spending, Republicans should force the issue of eliminating foreign aid. Fifty billion dollars in aid could be saved if this politically unpopular program were dropped. Even if legislators wanted to retain aid packages to the most troubled nations, the government could save billions by severing all other aid disbursements. Democrats would be hard pressed to win the support of the American people if they chose to save foreign aid spending while allowing the government to shut down for lack of funds.*

As the CR [Continuing Resolution, a temporary spending measure to allow government to remain open while cutting costs in the fiscal budget] talks between the House Republicans and the administration and Senate Democrats near their deadline [in early April 2011], the House negotiators should put America's foreign aid budget on the table.

With the Democrats reportedly willing to cut about half of the $61 billion the GOP has sought, much of the balance could come from a moratorium in paying out the $50 billion of foreign economic and military aid the United States dispenses every year. Rather than engage in a numerical debate, the Republicans should make the fight about whether to cut the foreign aid budget. Who will defend foreign aid when we have a $1.6 trillion deficit?

## Money That Could Be Saved Is Wasted on Aid

American foreign aid appropriations have escalated from about $20 billion in 2000 to $50 billion today. Almost every single nation on earth gets our foreign aid. The major recipients of the $35 billion in economic aid we dispense are: Afghanistan, $2.6 billion; Israel, $3 billion; Iraq, $766 million; and Egypt, $1.6 billion. But beyond these aid packages, we give Africa $7 billion in economic aid each year. We donate $2 billion to the Western Hemisphere (only about $400 million of it to Haiti). We give Asia, apart from Afghanistan, $2 billion. And we give Europe almost $1 billion.

---

*When Americans understand the extent to which we, as the nation running the largest budget deficit in the world, are subsidizing almost every other nation on the planet, their patience will be exhausted.*

---

Foreign aid has never been politically popular in the United States, and now is the time to put it on the table in the budget talks. If the Democrats want to shut down the government so that we can give more money in foreign aid, let them do it!

While it is true that much of the foreign aid we dispense goes to a few countries, almost everybody gets something. Aside from the major recipients (Israel, Egypt, Afghanistan, Pakistan and Iraq), many other nations get more than $100 million each year. . . .

When Americans understand the extent to which we, as the nation running the largest budget deficit in the world, are subsidizing almost every other nation on the planet, their patience will be exhausted.

## Cutting Aid or Shutting Down Government

Even if we hold apart from the proposed moratorium on foreign aid those nations currently in the midst of key foreign conflicts in which there is an American interest—Afghanistan, Iraq, Egypt and Israel—there is still a pool of upward of $30 billion from which to cut. With half the fiscal year remaining, a prorated cut of $15 billion would fill most of the gap between the House and Senate proposals for reduction of spending.

But the larger point is that House Republicans must put more than mere numbers in play in the debate with the administration and Senate Democrats. As pressing as the need to cut government spending and our budget deficit is, few will storm the barricades over the difference between $30 billion and $60 billion in budget cuts. But if the issue is whether to fund foreign aid to every nation on Earth, it becomes one that all can grasp, and the debate one in which all will participate—and not in a way to the Democrats' liking.

And, if the negotiations do not succeed and a government shutdown looms, just shut down the foreign aid budget. The House should pass the rest of the CR. Let the rest of the government operate as usual; just foreign aid will no longer be dispensed. Democrats cannot and will not trigger a general shutdown to protect the foreign aid budget, believe me.

# Aid to Nations

| | |
|---|---|
| Ivory Coast | $138M |
| Democratic Republic of the Congo | $213M |
| Ethiopia | $584M |
| Ghana | $175M |
| Kenya | $714M |
| Liberia | $219M |
| Malawi | $179M |
| Mali | $169M |
| Mozambique | $415M |
| Namibia | $103M |
| Nigeria | $648M |
| Rwanda | $241M |
| Senegal | $137M |
| South Africa | $586M |
| Sudan | $440M |
| Tanzania | $550M |
| Uganda | $480M |
| Zambia | $409M |
| Indonesia | $228M |
| Philippines | $133M |
| Vietnam | $123M |
| Ukraine | $124M |

5

# Congress Should Not Cut Foreign Aid

*Richard Stearns*

*A former businessman, Richard Stearns is president of World Vision, a Christian charity helping children and families overcome poverty worldwide. He is the author of* The Hole in Our Gospel, *a chronicle of his transition from business to charity work.*

*While Congress and presidential candidates bicker over how to cut federal spending, these politicians should refrain from cutting foreign aid. American food and monetary assistance helps save millions of lives around the globe and spreads the democratic ideals of this nation. Foreign aid is also an insignificant part of the federal budget and is not worth sacrificing if America wishes to retain its image of benevolence and moral certitude.*

I watched the Republican [presidential nomination] debates from my hotel in London this week [in October 2011], where I am meeting with other World Vision leaders. Being overseas, and watching them hours after the live event, provides a more objective perspective on home. During part of the discussion that evening, I found myself thinking: *This is not the America I love.*

One audience member asked a question on foreign aid. She said, "The American people are suffering in our country right now. Why do we continue to send foreign aid to other countries when we need all the help we can get for ourselves?"

Truthfully, this is a tough question. More Americans than ever since the Great Depression are out of work. Families have lost billions of dollars in net worth as their investment accounts have plummeted and housing values have sunk. Many people have lost their homes. Shouldn't we get our own house in order before trying to sweep up someone else's?

---

*The very real needs of Americans pale in comparison to the needs foreign aid addresses.*

---

## America Is Not Suffering Like the World's Poor

I have to be honest. While America's house needs a thorough spring cleaning, millions of the poor around the world are barely hanging on to survival, living in mud huts or under no roof at all. Those fleeing the famine now occurring in the Horn of Africa are building tents by tying pieces of cloth to sticks.

The very real needs of Americans pale in comparison to the needs foreign aid addresses. Poor families around the world are right now starving to death. If we cut American aid, we can be sure that millions will die. At a time when our politicians are considering how to cut as much as $1,500 billion from the federal budget we shouldn't try to cut the $16 billion we spend annually to assist the victims of malaria, famine, or natural disasters.

If I were advising the Republican candidates, I would encourage them to clear up some misperceptions about American foreign aid.

First, American aid is a small fraction of the US budget. Aid to the poor is less than 0.5 percent of the federal budget. It amounts to 14 cents per American per day. It hardly makes sense to think we can solve our fiscal problems by cutting funding to the poorest people in the world.

## The Benefits of Foreign Aid

Despite its small proportion to the budget as a whole, American aid is extremely effective. Three million people today are alive because of the PEPFAR AIDS program, which provides lifesaving drugs and 2.5 million AIDS orphans are being cared for. American assistance in the fight against malaria has saved an estimated 1 million lives. Preventable child deaths have declined from more than 20 million in 1960 to 7.6 million in 2010. Lives are at stake in this discussion.

*Money spent on foreign assistance for the poor is some of the most effective in the US budget. . . . Just because it's not perfect, doesn't mean we should stop doing it.*

Foreign aid promotes liberty and prosperity. A study of American assistance found that it led to increased democracy in the countries that received the aid. We are providing to others the freedoms we enjoy, allowing them to enjoy life, liberty and the pursuit of happiness. This wins America friends and creates goodwill. It even leads to jobs back home as half of US exports go to developing countries.

[Candidate] Ron Paul [a US Representative from Texas] was wrong when he said, "Foreign aid is taking money from poor people in this country and giving it to rich people in poor countries." Foreign aid isn't perfect, and not every dollar spent is as efficient as it could be. Solving poverty means dealing with a complex equation. But the money spent on foreign assistance for the poor is some of the most effective in the US budget. I've seen the rigorous controls our government has in place. Just because it's not perfect, doesn't mean we should stop doing it.

Doing good around the world is what I love about America. I have seen first-hand the incredible work our country does. I've seen the goodwill it builds. I have met people who are alive today because of American assistance. I believe in America, and that is why I believe in American aid.

## America Is a Land of Action and Moral Strength

In his parable of the Good Samaritan, Jesus told the story of the man who had compassion on the victim of robbers. While others passed by, Jesus commended the person who acted as a neighbor. "Go and do likewise," he said. (Luke 10:37)

Are we accurately reflecting our great nation if we simply pass the buck to others, with comments like, "We ought to get the Chinese to take care of the people," as one candidate said? We are not the kind of nation that asks others to do the hard work and to care for the most vulnerable. Throughout its history, American has acted as Good Samaritan, as neighbors, to the world.

Foreign aid isn't a campaign issue to bicker about. It's not an issue of left and right. It's about right and wrong. In the toughest times, the choices we make reflect our deepest character and values. Now, more than ever, the world needs America to go and do likewise.

# 6

# Congress Should Not Cut Millennium Challenge Corporation Funding

*James M. Roberts*

*James M. Roberts is a research fellow at the Center for International Trade and Economics at the Heritage Foundation, a conservative public policy think tank. Roberts's position at the foundation oversees the revising of the* Index of Economic Freedom, *the primary resource utilized by the Millennium Challenge Corporation (MCC) to determine whether a recipient nation is making progress toward governmental and economic freedom and thus merits MCC foreign aid.*

*As Congress seeks to cut federal spending and rein in the runaway budget, legislators should be careful in trimming foreign aid. While traditional foreign aid dispensed through USAID should be completely gutted because of its inability to effect measurable change in the well-being of recipient nations, some military aid, humanitarian aid, and especially aid provided through the Millennium Challenge Corporation should not be sacrificed. The Millennium Challenge Corporation—established in 2003— bypasses the failures of USAID by approving funding for projects in needy nations that demonstrate progress toward democratic reform and open trade policies. Holding these recipient nations accountable for wise spending and improved government means that aid money will be better used and have verifiable results. In reorganizing a new federal budget, Congress should not cut aid to this worthwhile program that benefits foreign populations and the interests of the United States.*

Congress faces many tough choices as it responds to the national security threat posed by out-of-control federal spending. However, the decision is easy in one area: foreign aid. Traditional development assistance does not work, at least not if the goal is to foster sustainable development in poor countries. Traditional efforts, such as those administered by the U.S. Agency for International Development (USAID), dole out billions of dollars each year despite evidence that these policies virtually ensure that economic growth will be minimal or unsustainable. Other types of U.S. foreign assistance—including security assistance, humanitarian assistance, and highly focused programs such as the President's Emergency Plan for AIDS Relief (PEPFAR)—are capable of achieving specific or short-term goals.

---

*As Congress considers ways to reduce the federal budget deficit, cuts to USAID and its traditional aid programs should be near the top of the list.*

---

The record of development assistance as a catalyst for long-term sustainable economic growth is abysmal. Perhaps the only exception to this poor track record is the Millennium Challenge Corporation (MCC), which requires countries to demonstrate foremost a commitment to good governance, sound economic policies, and the well-being of their citizens.

## Accountability Is the Key to Successful Aid

The MCC model holds recipient governments accountable for results and requires them to make serious, sustained efforts to combat corruption. MCC programs also encourage private-sector—led economic growth, strong protection of property rights, and the rule of law. All of these set the table for domestically driven economic growth and development, which can never be replaced by foreign assistance, no matter how well intentioned.

As a part of its foreign aid approval process, the MCC uses the trade freedom indicator in the *Index of Economic Freedom*, published annually by The Heritage Foundation and *The Wall Street Journal*. The entire MCC approach is consistent with the core values of the *Index*.

As Congress considers ways to reduce the federal budget deficit, cuts to USAID and its traditional aid programs should be near the top of the list. Other types of assistance—such as military assistance, humanitarian assistance, and MCC grants requiring policy reform—merit close scrutiny, but their past performance should justify continuing congressional support.

## Military Aid Enhances U.S. National Security

The value of U.S. international security assistance was illustrated most recently during the crisis in Egypt. The U.S. and Egyptian militaries have worked together closely for more than 30 years through such programs as the Foreign Military Sales (FMS) and International Military Education and Training (IMET) programs. When rioters on Tahrir Square demanded the overthrow of the [Hosni] Mubarak government last month [February 2011], it was Egypt's military—and only the military—that succeeded in holding the line against virulently anti-U.S. elements.

U.S. international security assistance has made direct and short-term contributions to America's national security and should continue to be funded. This assistance includes the FMS program to subsidize sales of U.S. military equipment, services, and training to friendly developing countries; IMET grants for training foreign military professionals; and some funding of international peacekeeping operations.

## PEPFAR: A Humanitarian Assistance Success Story

PEPFAR, the U.S. government's global effort to combat HIV/AIDS, is a recent example of the government's ability to respond effectively to a crisis when it wants to do so. PEPFAR has succeeded for a variety of reasons, but one of the most important was that its managers determined early on to focus on addressing one problem and to fence off its funding and management from USAID's ever-encroaching and entrepreneurial bureaucrats.

---

*Official development assistance (ODA) from USAID and other Western donor governments has a poor record of success in catalyzing economic growth and development.*

---

PEPFAR reflects a bipartisan political decision to apply a tangible and well-defined solution to solve a very real problem: namely, to design and implement systems to procure and deliver anti-retroviral HIV/AIDS drugs to those who are suffering from that disease around the world by using the latest generation of private business (not government) organizational techniques.

Other U.S. agencies have also led successful responses to humanitarian disasters (for example, earthquakes and tsunamis). One hallmark of these successes is that government delivery of humanitarian assistance was generally fenced off from USAID. This is powerful testimony to USAID's anachronistic ineffectiveness.

## Traditional Foreign Aid Programs Do Not Work

Official development assistance (ODA) from USAID and other Western donor governments has a poor record of success in catalyzing economic growth and development. Since 1960, developed member nations of the Organisation for Economic Co-operation and Development have donated more than $2 trillion in development assistance, but studies have shown that ODA failed to produce the desired results of job creation and higher living standards through economic growth.

The evidence indicates that this failure was preordained by the nature of ODA programs. Because ODA programs focus on government-to-government transfers, they tend to promote statist approaches to development among their recipients that enhance the power and size of recipient governments and create economic distortions in recipient economies. They also promote a welfare-dependency mindset and create new opportunities for corruption.

With rare exceptions, traditional aid ultimately reinforces the problems that contribute to a lack of development. Addressing such problems as illiteracy is important, but traditional development assistance programs aimed at such problems are too small to solve them and insufficient in themselves to overcome the policy impediments to economic growth.

Some USAID programs have devolved into little more than corporate welfare schemes for U.S. universities, nongovernmental organizations, and development assistance contractors. Members of Congress have commonly earmarked development assistance funds to benefit universities and contractors in their states.

---

*America should focus its development efforts on encouraging developing countries to improve their policies. Development assistance allocated with this objective should require far less funding while realizing far greater returns.*

---

Traditional development assistance is based on a world that no longer exists. In the 21st century, private financial flows from commerce and investment dwarf ODA levels. Every day, millions of private individuals, corporations, and other groups around the world demonstrate how the market creates the most efficient development strategies from knowledge shared through person-to-person contacts, phone calls, e-mails, and blogs—and, most important, from the technological knowledge and capital gained through trade and investment. Billions of dollars in private aid also flow annually to developing countries from faith-based and other charitable, academic, and humanitarian groups in developed countries. ODA cannot hope to compete.

The key is to facilitate these flows, not to compete with them. Private flows go where they can obtain the best return or can circumvent policy hurdles. America should focus its development efforts on encouraging developing countries to improve their policies. Development assistance allocated with this objective should require far less funding while realizing far greater returns.

## The MCC's Better Approach

Private-sector trade and investment is by far the best combination to spur sustainable economic growth in developing countries, and economic growth is the bedrock of economic freedom. Only a financially healthy private sector, operating in a competitive formal economy with secure property rights and transparent rule of law, can create the businesses and long-term jobs that are essential to long-term economic growth and development.

The MCC, created by Congress in 2003, was an innovative idea intended to overcome the shortcomings of the traditional USAID model and to encourage and allocate aid to countries that embrace policies linked to economic growth. The objective indicators used by the MCC to determine which countries will receive its funding—"based on their performance in governing justly, investing in their citizens, and encouraging economic freedom"—mirror those employed by The Heritage Foundation in preparing its *Index of Economic Freedom.*

---

*MCC's selectivity and associated seal of approval creates powerful incentives for developing countries to uphold democratic and free-market principles, invest responsibly in their citizens, and transition their economies from developing to emerging markets.*

---

A critical aspect of the MCC is its adherence to country ownership. Participation in MCC programs requires high-level engagement and commitment to transparency and accountability by the partner government, as well as by civil society and other domestic stakeholders. MCC programs focus on promoting sustainable economic growth to reduce poverty through projects in areas such as transportation, water and industrial infrastructure, agriculture, education, private-sector development, and capacity building.

MCC's selectivity and associated seal of approval creates powerful incentives for developing countries to uphold democratic and free-market principles, invest responsibly in their citizens, and transition their economies from developing to emerging markets. Development experts have approvingly labeled this the "MCC effect."

Focusing future taxpayer-funded U.S. government development assistance through the MCC will sustain a development approach that is more effective than the traditional aid model typified by USAID programs. The MCC's preliminary findings from its reviews of completed ("closed out") programs have been promising. For example, in Honduras, results from an agriculture training program show that annual incomes of farmers assisted by the MCC compact have increased from approximately $1,880 per hectare to $3,550 per hectare after two years of assistance. This gain of 88 percent greatly exceeds the 7 percent to 11 percent growth that would have been expected without the program.

## Congress Should Cut Traditional Aid

Traditional development assistance as delivered in past decades by USAID has largely failed to fulfill its stated goals. H.R. 1 (the continuing resolution) includes a 29 percent cut in fiscal year (FY) 2011 funding of MCC and a 30 percent cut for USAID.

Instead, per Heritage Foundation analyst Brian Riedl's recommendation, Congress should eliminate USAID's entire Development Assistance Program (currently $2.6 billion). This, along with Riedl's other recommended cuts in USAID's budget, would save $4 billion.

The MCC was an innovative idea to overcome the shortcomings of traditional development assistance, and the evidence since it was created eight years ago is promising. Rather than targeting the MCC—the most market-oriented of America's foreign aid programs—Congress should focus its development assistance cuts on the traditional USAID model that has repeatedly failed to deliver sustained economic growth and development.

# 7

# Foreign Aid Is Wasted on Africa

*Charles Abugre*

*Charles Abugre is a Ghanaian development economist. He currently heads the United Nations (UN) Millennium Campaign in Africa, a global advocacy arm of the UN that encourages developing nations and donors to meet poverty-reduction goals by 2015.*

*Foreign assistance to African nations has not proved very successful in enhancing development. Autocrats and corrupt African regimes have squandered aid money or spent it on projects that do not benefit the people. Aid funds should be given to those African countries working to end corruption and poverty, but they should not continue to enrich the coffers of dependent dictators. All Africans, however, should stand up and begin working for change—saving, investing, and bringing their expertise to bear on local programs. Only the African people can bring prosperity to their communities because aid money has failed to achieve this goal.*

I once asked a president of the Central African Republic, Ange-Félix Patassé, to give up a personal monopoly he held on the distribution of refined oil products in his country.

He was unapologetic. "Do you expect me to lose money in the service of my people?" he replied.

That, in a nutshell, has been the problem of Africa. Very few African governments have been on the same wavelength as Western providers of aid.

---

*Where [foreign aid] works, it represents only a very small share of the total resources devoted to improving roads, schools, heath services, and other things essential for raising incomes.*

---

Aid, by itself, has never developed anything, but where it has been allied to good public policy, sound economic management, and a strong determination to battle poverty, it has made an enormous difference in countries like India. Indonesia, and even China.

Those examples illustrate another lesson of aid. Where it works, it represents only a very small share of the total resources devoted to improving roads, schools, heath services, and other things essential for raising incomes.

Aid must not overwhelm or displace local efforts; instead, it must settle with being the junior partner.

## Too Much Aid, Too Little Wisdom

Because of Africa's needs, and the stubborn nature of its poverty, the continent has attracted far too much aid and far too much interfering by outsiders.

From the start, Western governments tried hard to work with public agencies, but fairly soon ran up against the obvious limitations of capacity and seriousness of African states.

Early solutions were to pour in "technical assistance," i.e. foreign advisers who stayed on for years, or to try "enclave" or turn-key projects that would be independent of government action.

More recently, Western agencies have worked with nongovernment organizations or the private sector. Or, making a virtue of necessity, they have poured large amounts of their assistance directly into government budgets, citing the need for "simplicity" and respect for local "sovereignty."

Through all of this, the development challenge was always on somebody else's shoulders and governments have been eager receivers, rather than clear-headed managers of Western generosity.

---

*Most African governments remain stuck in a culture of dependence or indifference.*

---

In the last 20 years, some states—like Ghana, Uganda, Tanzania, Mozambique, and Mali—have broken the mould, recognized the importance of taking charge, and tried to use aid more strategically and efficiently. Some commentators would add Benin, Zambia, and Rwanda to that list.

But most African governments remain stuck in a culture of dependence or indifference. There are still too many dictators in Africa (six have been in office for more than 25 years) and many elected leaders behave no differently.

## Creating the Right Climate for Progress

In Zambia last year [2009], journalist Chansa Kabwela sent photographs of a woman giving birth on the street outside a major hospital (where she had been refused admission) to the president's office, hoping he would look into why this had happened.

Instead, the president, Rupiah Banda, ordered the journalist prosecuted for promoting pornography. She was later acquitted.

Government callousness is one thing. Discouraging investors is even worse. No aid professional ever suggested that outside help was more important than private effort; on the contrary, foreign aid was intended to help lay the foundations for greater public confidence and private savings and investment.

Few economists thought that aid would create wealth, although most hoped that it would help distribute the benefits of growth more evenly. It was plain that institutions, policy, and individual effort were more important than money.

---

*An obvious solution is to focus aid on the small number of countries that are trying seriously to fight poverty and corruption.*

---

So, where—despite decades of aid—the conditions for private savings and investment are still forbidding, it is high time we ask ourselves why we are still trying to improve them.

The Blair Commission Report on Africa in 2005 reported that 70,000 trained professionals leave Africa every year, and until they—and the 40 percent of the continent's savings that are held abroad—start coming home, we need to use aid more restrictively.

An obvious solution is to focus aid on the small number of countries that are trying seriously to fight poverty and corruption. Other countries will need to wait—or settle with only small amounts of aid—until their politics or policies or attitudes to the private sector are more promising.

We should also consider introducing incentives for countries to match outside assistance with greater progress in raising local funds.

## Africans Must Act to Solve Their Own Problems

President [Barack] Obama is being criticized for increasing U.S. contributions to the international fight against HIV/AIDS by only two percent, with the result that people in Uganda are already being turned away from clinics and condemned to die.

When challenged, U.S. officials have had a fairly solid answer. Uganda has recently discovered oil and gas deposits but has gone on a spending spree, reportedly ordering fighter planes worth $300 million from Russia, according to a recent report in the *New York Times*.

Does a government that shows such wanton disregard for common sense or even good taste really have the moral basis for insisting on more help with AIDS?

We must not be distracted by recent news of Africa's "spectacular" growth and its sudden attractiveness to private investment. Some basic things are changing on the continent, with real effects for the future; above all, Africans are speaking out and refusing to accept tired excuses from their governments.

But the truth is that most of Africa's growth—based on oil and mineral exports—has not made a whit of difference to the lives of most Africans.

Political freedoms shrank on the continent last year, according to the U.S.-based Freedom House index.

A quarter of school-age children are still not enrolled, according to World Bank statistics; many of those that are, are receiving a very mediocre education. And agricultural productivity—the key to reducing poverty—is essentially stagnant.

The really good news is likely to stay local and seep out in small doses, until it eventually overwhelms the inertia and indifference of governments.

Five years ago, Kenya managed to double its tax revenues because a former businessman, appointed to head the national revenue agency, took a hatchet to the dishonest practices of many tax collectors. He had every reason to do so. Only five percent of Kenya's budget comes from foreign aid, compared with 40 percent in neighboring countries.

This is a good example of the sometimes-perverse effects of aid, but also of the importance of imagination and individual initiative in promoting a better life for Africans.

# 8

# US Foreign Aid Money Should Be Spent on America

*Gary Connor*

*A former reporter and veteran newsperson, Gary Connor is the publisher of the* Palestine Herald-Press, *a Texas newspaper.*

*The United States spends tens of billions of dollars each year on foreign aid. However, the same government that funds foreign regimes is forgetting to allocate enough money to tackle domestic problems. Disaster relief, school repair and rebuilding, and border security are underfunded, leaving American taxpayers to wonder why their money is being sent overseas. Before it decides to spend another dollar on foreign assistance, the US government should make sure it has adequately funded the domestic priorities that keep this nation safe, sound, and globally competitive.*

In the last two editions of the *Herald-Press* we have published information concerning the bureaucracy and megadollars the United States spends annually on foreign aid.

Congress has created 34 agencies dedicated to handing out your money and mine in the form of foreign aid. In FY2010 the feds gave away $39.4 billion in foreign assistance to 149 countries around the world.

We must insist Congress reduce the extravagant foreign aid spending and dedicate more funds to critical domestic needs including education, border security and domestic disaster relief.

Gary Connor, "U.S. Foreign Aid Series: America Should Come First," *Palestine (TX) Herald-Press*, June 21, 2011. Copyright © 2011 by the Palestine Herald-Press. All rights reserved. Reproduced by permission.

For instance, we recently published a request for monetary donations to reconstruct eight Joplin [Missouri] school campuses either destroyed or severely damaged by the recent EF5 tornado that devastated that community [in May 2011]. Construction costs are expected to top $150 million.

## America Is in Need of Foreign Aid Money

If the federal government transferred $20 million from each of the following nine countries' foreign aid for one fiscal year to the Joplin school rebuilding fund, the total would more than cover the construction costs: Mexico, Egypt, India, Bangladesh, Indonesia, Nigeria, South Africa, Zambia and Uganda. After the reduction of $20 million each, the foreign aid handed out to these particular countries would still range from $122 million (India) to $1.3 billion (Egypt).

---

*It seems more than simply ironic that while the federal government readily provides foreign assistance, victims of domestic disasters which fail to warrant the "national disaster" appellation, do not qualify for federal assistance.*

---

Educational facilities are not alone in their need for more federal funding. A news story last week reported a border patrol agent saying his agency is now apprehending illegal immigrants from many countries other than Mexico and Central America. He indicated the Texas, New Mexico and Arizona border with Mexico is now a doorway for not only Mexicans and Guatemalans, for instance, but also individuals from the Far East and the Middle East.

The porosity of this nation's southern border allows individuals with dishonorable intentions to walk into this country—in many cases to ride into this country—flooding our medical, educational and law enforcement services. Sooner or later one of these illegal immigrants will be a terrorist capable of causing great harm to Americans.

It seems more than simply ironic that while the federal government readily provides foreign assistance, victims of domestic disasters which fail to warrant the "national disaster" appellation, do not qualify for federal assistance. These disaster victims' only relief comes from organizations like the American Red Cross which operates strictly from volunteer donations and contributions.

The federal government should reduce foreign aid and increase funding for domestic disasters whether they are declared a "national disaster" or not. Our government should provide funding to help victims of all domestic disasters supporting the relief of human suffering within the borders of our nation.

## Taxpayers Should Demand That America Come First

When the president of the United States tells the American people the U.S. is going to pledge millions of dollars in foreign aid to an impoverished country, where does that money come from? That money, and all money the federal government spends (except what our nation's multi-trillion dollar spending forces us to borrow from China) comes from you and me, the American taxpayer. We are the government's revenue stream.

Isn't the rebuilding of the Joplin school system worthy of federal funding? Isn't protecting Americans from the onslaught of illegal immigrants deserving of federal funds? Shouldn't all victims of domestic disasters qualify for federal relief funds? The answer, of course, is an obvious "Yes!"

Before the federal government sends another $39.4 billion or more in foreign aid to its recipient countries around the world next year, it should be absolutely certain it has included adequate federal funds for education, border security and domestic emergency relief for American citizens and communities who are victims of national disasters.

America and Americans should come first.

# 9

# American Foreign Aid Supports Corrupt Regimes

*Thomas R. Eddlem*

*Thomas R. Eddlem hosts a radio talk show in the southeastern Massachusetts area. He is also a frequent contributor to* The New American, *a publication of the John Birch Society.*

*US foreign aid programs have often funded autocratic regimes that have committed human rights abuses and stand against democratic principles. In the wake of the 2010–2011 uprisings in various Arab nations, critics of foreign aid have pointed out how US dollars are propping up oppressive governments and funding the military forces that are called upon to beat down and otherwise control demonstrators. The federal government often excuses its aid packages to these Arab autocrats by insisting that these conflicted countries are strategic allies in the fight against terrorism, but it is difficult to reconcile anti-terrorism efforts and the detention, torture, and harassment of protestors who are clamoring for more open government. America must get wise to the fact that using foreign aid to support oppressive governments is not only unjust but is also earning the distrust and animosity of the masses who will ultimately overthrow the dictators and form new republics.*

Massive street protests erupted in Tunisia in late December [2010], which ended the 23-year reign of dictator Zine El Abidine Ben Ali. Fueled largely by an Internet-connected youth movement, the protests were partly a reaction to the publication by WikiLeaks of documents from U.S. diplomatic cables that revealed pandemic corruption by the ruling party, as well as government oppression that included arrests of lawyers, journalists, and political opponents. Another spark helped to ignite the revolt was the dramatic protest by Mohamed Bouazizi, who publicly set himself on fire on December 17 because of frequent government confiscation of his produce in his street vendor's business and the government's refusal to issue him the required vendor permits.

In the last weeks of January [2011], similar protests erupted across Egypt, forcing 30-year dictator Hosni Mubarak to appoint a new government and pledge not to run for another term when his current term expires in September. Massive protests have also spread to the Islamic nations of Jordan, Yemen, and Algeria. A movement similar to those happening in Tunisia and Egypt was put down by the Iranian government last spring [2010], but may rise up again at any moment.

---

*The recent events in the Islamic world have highlighted the reality that foreign aid has historically been used to suppress freedom and has reduced the moral influence of the example of the U.S. Constitution around the world.*

---

The Islamic dominoes appear to be falling, and a growing wired-in and educated Islamic middle class has made these protests for freedom possible. But what made these protests necessary? The simple answer is that the protests were necessary because the U.S. government propped up those corrupt regimes with massive amounts of foreign aid through the years. All of the governments mentioned above (except Iran) have been 30-year dynastic dictatorships backed by piles of U.S. foreign aid cash. The same U.S. foreign aid that backed the falling corrupt regimes is likely to reduce U.S. influence in those countries' new governments to zero.

## Arming Egyptian Oppressors

The State Department's *Quadrennial Diplomacy and Development Review* released last year claims that foreign aid give-aways are designed "to harness our civilian power to advance America's interests and help make a world in which more people in more places can live in freedom, enjoy economic opportunity, and have a chance to live up to their God-given potential." But the recent events in the Islamic world have highlighted the reality that foreign aid has historically been used to suppress freedom and has reduced the moral influence of the example of the U.S. Constitution around the world. Various news outlets have echoed precisely what David Reiff of *The New Republic* reported February 4: "U.S. military aid to Egypt—which averages $1.3 billion annually, and which this week allowed Egyptian police and paramilitaries to bombard protesters with volley after volley of tear gas made by Combined Systems International of Jamestown, Pennsylvania—may be grotesque in the objective sense because Washington has provided the Egyptian armed forces with such weapons platforms and systems as F-16 fighter aircraft, Abrams Main Battle Tanks, Apache attack helicopters, anti-aircraft missile batteries, and much else."

---

*American aid to Egypt has purchased over the past three decades a highly authoritarian regime that . . . engages in "routine and pervasive" torture and police brutality.*

---

The instruments of oppression used against freedom demonstrations in recent months have all been American-made and paid for by U.S. taxpayers. And this has been the case for decades. Rieff—no opponent of foreign aid in theory—

concluded of aid to Egypt, "This is not only a moral scandal, it is a geo-strategic blunder of huge proportions."

America has given Egypt $1.3 billion per year in military aid since the 1978 Camp David Accords, along with a comparable level of "development" aid, though development aid has been reduced in recent years. The "take" by the 30-year Mubarak regime from the U.S. taxpayer has been more than $60 billion, the second largest recipient of U.S. foreign aid over the same period.

American aid to Egypt has purchased over the past three decades a highly authoritarian regime that, according to classified U.S. diplomatic cables released by WikiLeaks, engages in "routine and pervasive" torture and police brutality. Those same secret U.S. diplomatic cables justified subsidizing the oppressive regime on the basis that aiding the dictatorship purchased peace between Egypt and Israel and won U.S. military overflight access. U.S. diplomats stressed in the cables: "Since our Foreign Military Financing (FMF) program began almost 30 years ago, our strong military relationship has supported peace between Egypt and Israel and ensured critical Suez Canal and overflight access for U.S. military operations."

---

*[US-funded] anti-terrorism training has a dual use [in oppressive states]: putting down democratic demonstrations.*

---

## Propping up Ben Ali in Tunisia

U.S. military aid also helped to train the oppressors of the people of Tunisia. According to the website of the U.S. embassy in Tunisia, the U.S. government offered the following military aid to the Ben Ali dictatorship:

- 8.5 million dollars in Foreign Military Finance (FMF) support in 2006. FMF is an ongoing program which helps to sustain and modernize Tunisia's military forces and equipment and enhances our overall military cooperation programs.

- The U.S. Department of Defense and the Tunisian Ministry of Defense cooperate as well in training and bilateral exercises including the U.S. Department of Defense "International Military Education and Training" (IMET) program which has trained over 3,600 Tunisian military officers/technicians since its inception in the mid-1980s. In 2005, 64 Tunisian military personnel were trained through the IMET program, at a value of $1.85M.

- Over the past several years, the Diplomatic Security branch of the U.S. Department of State sponsored a series of anti-terrorism training courses for Tunisian security officials. Over 300 Tunisian security officials have participated in courses including training in such areas as crisis response, explosive incidents countermeasures, airport security training, and anti-terrorism. Of course, anti-terrorism training has a dual use: putting down democratic demonstrations. And the U.S. State Department gave this aid despite its own report that concluded "security forces tortured detainees to elicit confessions and discourage resistance" and the fact that the government was a one-party state: "Tunisia is a republic with a strong presidential system dominated by a single political party. President Zine El Abidine Ben Ali has been in office since 1987. . . . The ruling party, the Democratic Constitutional Rally (RCD), was the sole legal party for 25 years—including when it was known as the Socialist Destourian Party (PSD)—and still dominates political life." The U.S. embassy nevertheless noted of the Ben Ali regime that "Tunisia is an important ally in the global war against terrorism."

"President" Ben Ali reportedly left the country January 14 after a month of ever-increasing protests, despite the words of encouragement, weapons, and training from the U.S. government.

## Subsidizing Autocracy in Jordan

Jordan has also erupted in massive upheaval, with protestors demanding political and economic freedoms. According to the State Department's own 2009 *Human Rights Report*, Jordan is a dictatorship led by a hereditary king, Abdullah II bin al-Hussein. Hussein is descended from the Islamic Prophet Muhammad's daughter Fatimah. The report notes that the Jordanian "constitution concentrates executive and legislative authority in the king." Therefore, "the government restricted citizens' right to change their government. . . . Torture remained a widespread practice . . . [and the] government controlled access to certain Internet content."

Yet Jordan, with a population of just six million, has been the recipient of more than half a billion dollars in U.S. aid annually since 2002, including both military and "development" aid. That's about $100 for every man, woman, and child in the country—every year.

---

*Foreign aid served as a cornerstone of making possible the September 11 attacks in New York City and Washington, D.C.*

---

## Corruption and Human Rights Abuses in Yemen

President Ali Abdullah Saleh has been "President" of Yemen since the unification of North and South Yemen in 1990. He was the "President" of Northern Yemen before that, beginning in 1978. The U.S. State Department's 2009 *Advancing Freedom and Democracy Reports* notes that the Yemeni government exhibits thorough "corruption, fraudulent voter registration, and administrative weakness. There were reports that government forces committed arbitrary and unlawful killings. Torture and poor conditions reportedly existed in prisons. Prolonged pretrial detention, judicial corruption, and executive interference continued to undermine due process. Arbitrary arrest and detention increased."

And yet the State Department openly admits "the United States works with government officials." That work includes military aid to support "stability" for the existing dictatorship, according to the U.S. State Department: "Defense relations between Yemen and the United States are improving rapidly, with the resumption of International Military Education and Training assistance and the transfer of military equipment and spare parts. In FY 2009 U.S. Foreign Military Financing (FMF) for Yemen was $2.8 million, International Military Education and Training (IMET) was $1 million, and Non-Proliferation, Anti-Terrorism, Demining and Related Programs (NADR) was $2.5 million. In FY 2009 Yemen also received $19.8 million in Economic Support Funds (ESF), $ 11.2 million in development assistance, and $67.1 million in Section 1206 funding." The State Department describes Yemen as "an important partner in counterterrorism efforts, providing assistance in the military, diplomatic, and counterterrorism finance arenas. Yemen has stepped up its counterterrorism cooperation efforts with the United States, achieving significant results and improving overall security in Yemen." But of course, the "security" and "stability" that the U.S. aid actually promoted was for Abdullah Saleh's hold on power over the Yemeni people. Yemen, a poor nation, has also seen massive protests against Abdullah Saleh's regime.

## Afghanistan Foreign Aid Led to 9/11

Foreign aid served as a cornerstone of making possible the September 11 attacks in New York City and Washington, D.C.

Military aid for the Afghan rebels against the Soviet Union in the 1980s helped bring the Taliban warlords to power. While *Time* magazine claimed in 2003 that [al Qaeda terrorist leader] Osama bin Laden was personally a recipient of Mujahedeen-bound U.S. taxpayer-provided weapons, this is unlikely. There wasn't any need for bin Laden to receive U.S. weapons, as he did little actual fighting and his role in Afghanistan was one of a supplier of weapons and materiel, using his own ample private funding from his family fortune in Saudi Arabia. But the CIA and bin Laden did fund the same Afghan rebel groups under Gulbuddin Hekmatyar and others that eventually became the Taliban.

Hekmatyar reportedly received $500 million in U.S. weapons and aid, funneled through the Pakistani intelligence service, the ISI. And other rebel groups that became part of the Taliban also received U.S. weapons. And these same Taliban groups that emerged as victors in the Soviet-Afghan war became the same Taliban that sponsored bin Laden's al-Qaeda organization after bin Laden's group was expelled from the Sudan in 1996.

---

*Of course, the foreign aid "investment" in foreign dictators around the world has often led American politicians and pontificators to cling to the dictators long after the people of their countries have any use for them.*

---

## Sticking with the Dictators

Tea Party favorite and freshman Kentucky Senator Rand Paul has proposed as part of the solution to the federal budget crisis that the federal government should end all foreign aid, telling CNN's Wolf Blitzer that the "American people agree with me that when we're short of money, where we can't do the things we need to do in our country, we certainly shouldn't be shipping the money overseas." A Reuters poll released earlier that week demonstrated 73 percent of the American people want to cut or eliminate foreign aid.

Neoconservative commentator David Frum—a fervent supporter of foreign aid—candidly admitted on his blog during the Egyptian protests, "The point of foreign aid is not economics; it is geopolitics: It is intended to shape a recipient country's behavior and, quite literally, buy American influence." Frum, like the [Barack] Obama administration, advocates that billions in aid continue to flow to Egypt because such largesse will increase the U.S. role as a power-broker just as the Egyptian people are about to throw off the corrupt regime.

Of course, the foreign aid "investment" in foreign dictators around the world has often led American politicians and pontificators to cling to the dictators long after the people of their countries have any use for them. Such has been the case with the Obama-Biden administration and the Mubarak regime in Egypt. A week after massive Egyptian protests in Tahrir Square made worldwide headlines, Secretary of State [Hillary] Clinton and Vice President [Joe] Biden told Americans they were sticking with the dictator. "I would not refer to him as a dictator." Biden said on PBS' *NewsHour* on January 27. Meanwhile, Clinton told David Gregory on NBC's *Meet the Press* that "President Mubarak and his government have been an important partner to the United States" and that the government was exercising "restraint" in its dealings with the demonstrators, even as beatings, shootings, and murders mounted. But reality did eventually set in. On February 6, long after it became obvious that a transition of power from Mubarak was going to happen anyway, President Obama finally told Fox News' Bill O'Reilly about Mubarak, "What we've said is you've got to lead to a transition now."

## Foreign Aid Is Buying Foreign Ill-Will

That's not to say the Obama administration has allowed too much reality to enter the public debate. The Obama administration's immediate plans include ramping up foreign aid giveaways. The State Department's *Quadrennial Diplomacy and Development Review* calls for creation of a host of new job positions and agencies, including "creating an Under Secretary for Civilian Security, Democracy, and Human Rights" and a "Coordinator for Cyber Issues," establishing "a Bureau of Policy, Planning, and Learning" and a "Bureau for Counterterrorism," and appointing "a Global Food Security Coordinator" and "a new Bureau for Energy Resources." The phrases "abolish" and "phase out" for other agencies or officers already tasked with similar foreign aid and foreign manipulation appear nowhere in the document.

Considering the bloody history of foreign aid, and the current prospects of some major political blow-back caused by U.S. government past backing of dictators with foreign aid money, Senator Rand Paul may have expressed only part of the problem with foreign aid. Americans are paying the monetary cost of foreign aid out of their wallets, but they are also paying another—higher—cost for the ill-will that our foreign aid has created for America abroad. Even if the federal government were enjoying an embarrassing budget surplus, as it did during much of the 19th century, Americans still couldn't afford the cost of foreign aid.

# 10

# America Should Aid Nations That Demonstrate Governmental Accountability

*Larry Diamond*

*A professor by courtesy of political science and sociology at Stanford University, Larry Diamond is a senior fellow at the Hoover Institution, a public policy think tank that supports private enterprise and personal freedom. Diamond is the founding co-editor of the* Journal of Democracy *and is the author of* The Spirit of Democracy: The Struggle to Build Free Societies throughout the World *and other books.*

*The Millennium Challenge Account (MCA) and the organization that oversees it, the Millennium Challenge Corporation, have shown some success in allocating aid to developing countries on the condition that these countries improve their rule of law. However, the MCA still tends to offer money to countries that are making dismal progress as long as some progress is made. America should restructure all of its aid programs around the MCA model but further restrict all aid appropriations, giving only to nations that are proving accountable and open to democratic and market changes. In this way, foreign nations will not simply remain dependent on US welfare; they will compete for aid and demonstrate significant changes in order to win funding. Such a transition will benefit American funding policy and help bring freedom and trade to deserving people around the globe.*

Larry Diamond, "End Foreign Aid As We Know It," *Democracy: A Journal of Ideas*, No. 8, 2008. www.democracyjournal.org. Copyright © 2008 by Democracy: A Journal of Ideas. All rights reserved. Reproduced by permission.

After more than four decades and $500 billion in international aid, much of Africa remains as poor, if not worse off, than it was at independence. The same is true around the world: Aid flows profusely to governments with little or no inclination to control corruption and reduce poverty. Despite tough talk about "good governance," it is still largely business as usual: predatory governments pretend to be promoting development, and the donors profess to be aiding it. The losers are the people of these so-called "developing countries," who lack the schools, clinics, medicines, roads, housing, irrigation, sanitation, drinking water, credit, and justice that they need to be productive—or even survive.

---

*There is no coherent strategy to demand that countries construct strong institutions of accountability to uncover and punish corruption.*

---

## Selective Aid Based on Competition and Accountability

More money is not the answer. It's time to end foreign aid as we know it. We can begin by building on one of President George W. Bush's few good initiatives, the Millennium Challenge Account (MCA), which operates on the basis of incentives and "selectivity." Low- and lower-middle-income countries compete for sizeable increases in aid on the basis of three criteria: ruling justly (by providing freedom and a rule of law and by controlling corruption); investing in people (especially basic health and education); and promoting economic freedom. Sixteen publicly available indicators, drawn from independent agencies, are used to measure the criteria, and are applied in a reasonably fair and independent fashion.

But these new principles still govern only a small proportion of overall U.S. foreign aid, much of which continues to flow to deeply corrupt governments. Moreover, MCA assistance is not without its flaws. It is awarded on a curve so if most of the potential recipients have high levels of corruption and malfeasance, the aid simply goes to the "less bad." And there is no coherent strategy to demand that countries construct strong institutions of accountability to uncover and punish corruption. In addition, while other donors are gingerly moving toward good governance standards, only the United States has established an entire aid program based on these principles. Finally, the Millennium Challenge Corporation, which disburses MCA funds, has been too hung up negotiating the details of country assistance projects, and thus slow to send money.

---

*Countries serious about governance and development . . . should get substantial aid increases. Venal governments should be largely cut off.*

---

## Give Funds Only to Those Governments Showing Good Governance

So what next? First, apart from public health and urgent humanitarian aid, the American foreign aid budget (which totaled $23.5 billion in 2006) should be reorganized around MCA principles, with a particular emphasis on institutions to control corruption. Countries serious about governance and development—as measured without a curve—should get substantial aid increases. Venal governments should be largely cut off (unless the president signs and Congress approves a waiver for explicit national security reasons). Each country should come up with its own reform plan, as a result of free and vigorous discussion. However, any credible plan must include some key components: a free press; an independent judiciary; and robust institutions of accountability such as a counter-corruption commission, an ombudsman, and audit agencies. All of these must have the leadership, legal authority, and resources to monitor official conduct and probe and punish wrongdoing. Once they are established and given the necessary authority, the donors should provide generous financial and technical assistance to help train and equip them.

---

*The whole logic of global aid institutions has to change, so that officials are rewarded for stimulating real development, not for pushing money out the door.*

---

Second, the practice of relieving the debts of bad governments, only to have them pile up fresh debt in new frenzies of corruption, should end. Future debts of low-income countries should not be forgiven in one fell swoop, but suspended and retired incrementally (for example, at 10 percent annually for every year that countries adhere to good-governance standards).

Third, we need to fight for aid accountability globally. We should push Europe, Japan, and the World Bank to also reorganize their own aid programs. And the next administration should press the World Bank for radical reform of its structures and practices, both to root out corruption in its own projects and to insist on better governance as a condition for aid. The whole logic of global aid institutions has to change, so that officials are rewarded for stimulating real development, not for pushing money out the door.

## Restructure USAID

Finally, we need a fundamental reorganization of our own institutions to promote development. In its current understaffed, over-bureaucratized, demoralized state—with heavy reliance on for-profit corporations to implement its programs—the U.S. Agency for International Development [USAID] cannot be the agent of a global "new deal" for development. It should become a cabinet-level Department of International Development and Reconstruction, with a dramatic expansion of career staff (back to the levels of the 1960s), enhanced democracy and governance assistance programs, and more capacity to move quickly into changing circumstances with diffuse engagement and small grants.

In the world's poorest countries, poor people and their civil societies know that aid will not bring development without accountability and a rule of law. The next American president can win their hearts and change their minds about America—and improve our own security—by showing that we agree.

# 11

# America Should Aid Nations That Show Progress Toward Goals

*Nancy Birdsall, Ayah Mahgoub, and William D. Savedoff*

*Nancy Birdsall is the founding president of the Center for Global Development (CGD), a nonprofit organization that seeks to end global poverty by advocating for just governmental policy measures. Ayah Mahgoub is Program Coordinator at the CGD, and William D. Savedoff is a CGD research fellow.*

*Traditional aid models are based on funding a need and hoping for the best outcome. In such cases, disinterest, corruption, and a host of other complaints can derail aid money from achieving its goal. To make the process more transparent, the US government and other interested aid foundations should adopt a "cash on delivery" (COD) model. Under a COD program, funders would pay for verifiable results. Thus, aid recipients would define a need, offer a solution, and achieve the outcome before aid was disbursed. This experiment offers strong incentives for recipients to bring about the needed change, and it gives some form of guarantee to the funders that their money is paying for results. Obviously, because COD aid is distributed at various points of progress, it should work along with other forms of aid that can fund projects from the start. However, COD aid can encourage results and perhaps encourage more donors to participate once they are assured that their money will be well spent.*

Critics of foreign aid contend that much of it is ineffective or even hinders development. They argue that risk aversion—being concerned more with disbursing funds than achieving results—discourages local innovation and that a presumption that funders and their professional staff know which strategies will succeed discourages local learning. They maintain as well that the aid system is cumbersome, costly to administer, difficult to explain, and rarely transparent.

These and other problems have encouraged the donor community to emphasize country ownership and promote results-based programs. These changes are in response to a fundamental challenge: foreign aid fosters a nontransparent relationship of accountability between recipients and foreign funders that undermines accountability between governments and their own citizens. With weak local accountability and pressure from their own taxpayers and contributors, funders try to control the use of their assistance, often by financing and monitoring inputs, which are easier and quicker to track than outcomes. Funders that try to channel aid on the basis of results are often forced to backtrack in the face of objections: that giving local governments discretion will facilitate corruption; that it takes too long for results to be manifest; that it is too costly or difficult to measure outcomes. Consequently, funders end up buying things instead of buying development.

---

*Cash on Delivery Aid builds on other approaches that have pushed toward increasing country ownership and paying for results.*

---

International agreements such as the Paris Declaration and Accra Agenda for Action call for a number of things that would characterize more effective aid: a focus on results, more predictable aid, improved accountability, greater country ownership, and harmonization of foreign assistance approaches. However, these agreements don't provide practical mechanisms to achieve these aims.

## The Cash on Delivery Approach

Cash on Delivery [COD] Aid builds on other approaches that have pushed toward increasing country ownership and paying for results. It is designed to strengthen the accountability of recipient governments to their citizens, funders to recipient governments, and recipient governments to funders by making financing contingent upon transparent and measurable incremental progress on specific shared goals. The novelty of COD Aid is in the combination of five basic features: payments for outcomes, hands-off implementation, independent verification of progress, transparency through public dissemination, and complementarity with other aid programs.

*Payments for Outcomes, Not Inputs.* First, the funder pays for an outcome, not an input, agreeable to both the recipient and funder. The outcome must be measurable and should be continuous (such as number of children enrolled in school or surviving to age five), making it possible to pay in proportion to progress.

---

*Giving governments the flexibility to design and implement policies and programs promotes country ownership and allows them to build their own capacity and make full use of local knowledge and experiences to innovate and learn.*

---

There are several benefits to providing aid in this way. It helps funders show measurable results to their constituents. It enables funders to complement existing projects and programs of support in countries that may not be eligible to receive budget support. It also creates incentives to collect reliable performance information, whereas traditional aid forces recipients to spend time on detailed reporting of expenditures and activities. Finally, the data produced under a COD Aid program help policymakers and researchers learn which programs are effective and why.

*Hands-off Funders and Responsible Recipients.* Second, the funder embraces a hands-off approach, affirming recipients' responsibility and authority to implement development programs in their country. The funder does not pay for inputs and entirely eschews designing or demanding any particular new intervention or investments. The recipient in turn has complete discretion over the chosen strategy. Furthermore, the recipient can use the funds if receives after making progress in any way it chooses. This hands-off feature distinguishes COD Aid sharply from most existing aid modalities and reduces administrative costs considerably.

Giving governments the flexibility to design and implement policies and programs promotes country ownership and allows them to build their own capacity and make full use of local knowledge and experiences to innovate and learn. Recipients can request technical assistance, ideas, and guidance from funders. Such technical help, being demand-driven, is more likely to be used well.

---

*We believe that COD Aid can and should be introduced as an addition to current aid flows without disrupting ongoing programs.*

---

*Independent Verification.* Third, COD Aid requires independent verification of progress toward the agreed-upon outcome. While recipients are responsible for measuring and reporting their progress, independent verification—based on new information obtained by a third party independent of the recipient—is critical to the credibility of the agreement. Obtaining such information is also the only way for recipients to accurately assess and improve their reporting systems. Funders should pay for the costs of independently verifying the measure of progress.

*Transparency through Public Dissemination.* Fourth, COD Aid transparently and publicly disseminates the content of the

COD Aid contract itself, the amount of progress, and the payments. To encourage public scrutiny and understanding, the indicator or measure of progress should be as simple as possible. Simplicity and transparency increase the credibility of the arrangement, help ensure that the parties fulfill their commitments, improve accountability to the public, and encourage broader social engagement in aspects of progress beyond the specific object of the contract. Public access to information about a government's progress could enable civil society to hold the government to account for the quality and quantity of its services.

*Complementarity with Other Aid Programs.* Fifth, COD Aid complements other aid programs. We believe that COD Aid can and should be introduced as an addition to current aid flows without disrupting ongoing programs. Indeed, we argue that COD Aid would create healthy incentives for funders and recipients to use existing resources more efficiently. Over time, recipients and funders can assess the COD Aid mechanism and its effectiveness relative to other aid mechanisms.

## Application to Primary Education

The most common objection to COD Aid is that it is not practical. To assess this objection, we convened experts and policymakers to help us design a COD Aid program in primary education. We chose primary education in part because governments and funders have already publicly committed to a shared goal: one of the eight Millennium Development Goals [development goals agreed upon by committed UN member states that are designed to be reached by 2015] is universal primary school completion. The resulting proposal outlined below is explained in detail in our book, *Cash on Delivery: A New Approach to Foreign Aid with an Application to Primary Schooling.*

Under our proposal, the unit of progress would be an "assessed completer," a student enrolled in the last year of primary school who takes an approved standardized assessment exam. The funder would agree to pay $20 for each assessed completer up to the total enrollment in the base year and $200 for each assessed completer in excess of that number. The recipient would commit to disseminating its information on student enrollments, assessed completers, and test scores. The funder would commit to contracting a third party to verify the accuracy of the recipient's reports. Payments would be offered for assessed completers regardless of their test scores to limit incentives to misreport progress—a recurring problem associated with high-stakes testing worldwide. Public dissemination of student achievement would equip governments and civil society with information about schooling quality and help them learn which schools work.

---

*In contrast to most sector- and budget-support programs, a COD Aid agreement would increase transparency by linking funds to a single, easily understood, and credible indicator of real progress.*

---

In contrast to traditional education programs, COD Aid funds would give whole governments an incentive to tackle all kinds of constraints on educational progress, many of them outside the education system itself, whether that requires simplifying financial administration to disburse funds on time, assuring good transportation and reliable electricity to reach schools, or linking antipoverty programs to school attendance. It provides the government with room to involve the private sector and experiment with vouchers or new regulatory approaches. In contrast to most sector- and budget-support programs, a COD Aid agreement would increase transparency by linking funds to a single, easily understood, and credible indicator of real progress. The need to accurately measure primary completion would foster demand for the collection of accurate, comprehensive data on student achievement. The availability of the data would enable civil society to hold the government to account for providing good education; it would also provide better information for policymakers.

## COD Aid for Other Development Goals

A COD Aid program can be designed to attain any shared goals for which measurable progress can be defined. Possibilities include expanding secondary education, increasing immunization coverage, preventing the spread of HIV/AIDS, expanding access to running water, and slowing deforestation. To design new applications of COD Aid, funders and recipient governments would agree on a goal, identify an appropriate outcome measure, set a fee per unit of progress, and establish a way to report and verify progress.

## Managing Risk

As with all initiatives, COD Aid agreements entail risks. We recognize three categories: those that can be managed through program and contract design, those that are associated with all forms of aid, and those related to misconceptions and departures from current practice. We discuss each below. . . .

---

*COD Aid can be more successful in the face of corruption than traditional aid because it is paid against verified progress while traditional aid disburses against documented expenditures regardless of progress.*

---

*Risks That Can Be Managed through Program and Contract Design.* Certain concerns can be managed during the program design and contract negotiation phase. One common concern is the *difficulty of measuring outcomes.* Program designers can minimize this concern by consulting with experts to determine an appropriate indicator for the shared goal. Incorporating independent verification, with an appropriate system of penalties for misrepresentation, can minimize the risk of over-reporting.

*Risks Associated with All Forms of Aid That Are Not Specific to COD Aid.* Many concerns about COD Aid are not unique to the approach. Government officials might *use the funds for illegitimate purposes*, for example, but all aid is vulnerable to corruption—even aid from programs that strictly monitor spending. COD Aid can be more successful in the face of corruption than traditional aid because it is paid against verified progress while traditional aid disburses against documented expenditures regardless of progress.

*Misconceptions and Departures from Current Practice.* A common misconception is that COD Aid subjects recipients to *greater unpredictability in aid flows*. In fact, COD Aid is more predictable than traditional aid flows, which are subject to shifting domestic political priorities in donor countries. The variability of COD Aid payments is associated with factors that are more under the control of the recipient (i.e., policies that affect outcomes).

---

*Once a COD Aid model agreement has been designed, any number of funders (whether public or private) can join without any additional negotiations.*

---

One common discomfort with COD Aid has to do with *not paying countries that fail to make progress*. Many results-oriented funders are in fact compromised by strong incentives to disburse money regardless of progress. Adopting a COD Aid approach demonstrates a strong commitment to pay only in proportion to success.

## Funding and Implementing COD Programs

The shift from monitoring inputs to paying against outcomes allows COD Aid agreements to be relatively simple and allows funders to coordinate their assistance at very low cost.

Once a COD Aid model agreement has been designed, any number of funders (whether public or private) can join without any additional negotiations. Funders could be official donors, private foundations, NGOs [nongovernmental organizations], multilateral institutions, or collaborations. If the agreement were offered to eligible countries as an "open contract," provisions would be necessary to limit the funders' exposure, either by restricting the contract to a specific number of countries or establishing a maximum payout. As more funders join, the arrangement could accommodate more countries.

A COD Aid program can be offered to any interested country (or subnational entity) that meets basic eligibility criteria, which if possible should be restricted to the conditions necessary for measuring and verifying the outcome indicator. For example, our education proposal would require a primary completion exam of acceptable quality. Funders can identify interested countries and engage in country-by-country negotiations, or they can offer an open contract. The latter is more attractive because it would reduce administrative costs, increase transparency through simplicity and uniformity, enhance fairness by valuing outcomes equally across countries, and encourage self-selection of countries for which the terms would be most attractive (e.g., a fixed amount per child would be relatively more attractive to poorer countries).

Funders may face a number of obstacles to enter long-term agreements that pay for results and dispense with the usual forms of analysis, negotiation, approval, and monitoring. However, funders have shown the capacity to innovate. The creation of the Millennium Challenge Corporation [A US aid program created in 2004 to target aid to countries that show progress toward good governance] and multi-year budget support partnership agreements are testaments to such efforts.

Once funders have committed to undertake a COD Aid program, funders and recipients can take the following steps to implement an agreement:

1. *Convene potential funders and recipients to review and negotiate a contract with the assistance of technical experts.* The group would specify an outcome indicator, establish eligibility criteria, establish the amount paid per unit of progress, and set a procedure for contracting an independent firm or university to conduct to verify results.

2. *Funders and recipients establish an institutional arrangement for receiving contributions and implementing the agreement.* The agreement could be implemented by a multilateral development bank that creates a special trust fund or by an independent nonprofit organization created especially for the purpose. The entity would sign contracts with contributors to receive funds or guarantees and be responsible for contracting with agents to verify results, assure compliance with the contract, and make payments as progress occurs. It would be empowered to sign binding credible agreements with developing countries, with the financial backing to make payments in the future in accordance with progress.

3. *Elicit interest from recipient countries.* Countries that meet the basic eligibility criteria would enter discussions about the kinds and quality of information they have available to implement the agreement. If testing and verification methods were in place, a country could sign the agreement, establish a baseline, and implement its strategy. If testing and verification were not acceptable, the funder could offer technical assistance to meet these basic conditions.

4. *Evaluate the pilot experiences.* COD Aid is a significant departure from current approaches and should therefore be assessed carefully. Funders and recipients should work with an independent group to design an evaluation that would accompany the COD Aid agreement.

Funders would finance the evaluation, while the country would provide researchers with access to information.

Once the agreement is signed, the recipient would pursue its strategy and collect and report data on the outcomes as agreed in the contract. The funder would arrange for an audit of the report by the designated third party and, once the results are verified, disburse payments to the recipient.

## An Experiment Worth Trying

Despite its successes, foreign aid is subject to major critiques that it can be ineffective or even undermine development in recipient countries. COD Aid is an approach that could address these concerns by fully incorporating the principles of country ownership and paying for results. The simplicity of the approach—paying in proportion to progress that is independently verified—enhances its transparency and could contribute to a substantial improvement in accountability relationships among funders, recipients, and their respective constituencies. We do not pretend that COD Aid is a panacea for problems in the aid system but believe it holds enough promise to be worth trying, adapting, and assessing.

# 12

# Foreign Aid Should Focus on Strengthening Local Institutions

*Nicholas Eberstadt and Carol C. Adelman*

*Nicholas Eberstadt is the Henry Wendt Scholar in Political Economy at American Enterprise Institute, an organization of scholars that promotes free enterprise and individual liberty. Carol C. Adelman is the director of the Center for Global Prosperity at the Hudson Institute, a conservative think tank. Adelman was co-vice chairman and Eberstadt was commissioner of the US Helping to Enhance the Livelihood of People around the Globe Commission, a congressional assembly that met in 2006 and 2007 to examine US foreign aid and offer advice on improving assistance programs.*

*The dominant US foreign aid model is obsolete. Providing large sums to address various problems is not effective in modern times. America should tightly focus its aid to respond to local needs, whether supplying bed nets to regions plagued by malaria or building schools to educate future generations. To incorporate this new model, the United States should take advantage of local leaders who have experience in defining a need and have shown a commitment to solving problems. It should also work with nongovernmental institutions that have an interest in achieving results at the local level, and it should foster private enterprise*

Nicholas Eberstadt and Carol C. Adelman, "Foreign Aid: What Works and What Doesn't," *American Enterprise Institute Policy Outlook*, vol. 3, October 2008. Copyright © 2008 by the American Enterprise Institute. All rights reserved. Reproduced by permission.

*where it can. The most important factor in this new agenda is to build self-reliance and sustainability in communities so that aid dependency will end.*

Like many other bureaucratic organizations, foreign aid institutions are geared to fighting the last war—in this context, to meeting the development challenges of a world we no longer inhabit. Social, economic, and demographic changes in the developing world over the past several decades have been rapid, and they have transformed the low-income landscape in obvious respects, but these realities have yet to be internalized by many of our international development assistance agencies and programs. There are not just new problems to be faced. There are important new opportunities to be grasped. Three major, ongoing changes need to be recognized immediately, and they relate to demographics, health, education, and finance in the developing world.

---

*The rise in [the] pool of trained professionals and entrepreneurs in developing countries means that there are steadily increasing opportunities for aid organizations to partner with local talent.*

---

## Significant Changes in Developing Nations and Aid Funding

First, in much of the developing world, especially in Latin America and Asia, economic and demographic changes—including declining fertility and infant mortality and rising life expectancy—are producing a "grayer" population structure and more affluent populations. These trends have tilted the locus of health problems in most developing countries toward such chronic illnesses as cancer, cardiovascular disease, and diabetes, and away from the traditional problems of infectious diseases and child survival. While "traditional" health problems are still predominant in sub-Saharan countries, the chronic disease burden is increasingly significant even in Africa, affecting the working-age population so vital to productivity and growth.

Second, there has been an increase in the skill-based talent pool as millions of people who have studied in developed countries have returned home to start businesses and NGOs [nongovernmental organizations]. The rise in this pool of trained professionals and entrepreneurs in developing countries means that there are steadily increasing opportunities for aid organizations to partner with local talent. They have an enhanced opportunity to promote "local ownership," self-reliance, and sustainability through their projects.

---

*Economic growth in emerging economies has been creating considerable wealth, and that wealth is itself local.*

---

Finally, there are major streams of international financial resources available today (some of them entirely new) that were not present when foreign assistance was conceived after World War II. Some 77 percent of total financial flows from the developed to the developing world are private resources in the form of investment, remittances, and philanthropy. These private flows now dwarf government aid to the developing world. Most important, they have opened up entirely new ways of addressing problems. Increasingly, private philanthropists are taking a venture-capitalist approach to aid, viewing themselves as problem-solvers and partners rather than as donors simply providing transfers to recipients. Private resources are flowing through new channels: the Internet, mobile-phone transfers, cause-related marketing, remittances, and social networking sites. Economic growth in emerging economies has been creating considerable wealth, and that wealth is itself local. Large NGOs, such as the Aga Khan Foundation (which focuses on needs in South Asia, Central Asia, and eastern Africa), have now been joined by thousands of community foundations in the developing world that are solving local problems with local funding from wealthy individuals and companies.

What differs now is not only the nature of the problems in developing countries, but also the unprecedented array of new options for speeding up the tempo of material advance and the spread of prosperity. These changes call for a new business model for moving foreign aid resources. This model will require much more flexibility in aid programming in order to avoid "one size fits all" solutions for a diverse world, and it should be tailored to each country's evolving conditions and development opportunities. It should also be premised on leverage—that is, linking U.S. public resources to the myriad emerging streams of private endeavor that characterize global development and encouraging the emergence of more innovative and efficient ways of delivering assistance and better evaluating the aid's ultimate impact. . . .

---

*[Analysts] found that successful [aid] projects involved local initiative, good governance, measured results, and the creation of local institutions for sustainability.*

---

## A Shift from Macro-Level Aid to Local Aid

Since recipient countries' policies are almost always far more important than the volume of foreign assistance in hastening the pace of material advance in recipient countries, we need to ask: where and how can foreign aid matter? This requires a shift in focus from the macro level to the micro level, to projects on the ground. From the nearly $2.7 trillion in official development assistance transferred to recipient countries since 1960, what evidence of program-level success do we have? And why have the projects been successful? Even if the macroeconomic impact of aid transfers has been debatable, aid projects could still be justified by policymakers, and perhaps even by taxpayers, if they have generated high and sustained returns for their beneficiaries in low-income countries. Determining these characteristics of how foreign aid has positively affected the lives of individuals and communities in poor countries can inform our approach to future aid programs.

In recent years, many bilateral donors have examined the effectiveness of their foreign assistance. By and large, their findings have not been encouraging. In its stark evaluation of Canadian foreign aid, the Canadian Senate's Foreign Affairs Committee concluded that the Canadian International Development Agency has failed to make a difference in sub-Saharan Africa, despite $12.4 billion in aid expenditures between 1968 and 2007. The failure was attributed to slow, unaccountable, and poorly designed development assistance and ineffective foreign aid institutions in Africa. Maintaining that vibrant economies and good governance are the answer to prosperity and that these can only be generated from within African countries themselves, the committee recommended that Canada move to a foreign aid model similar to the U.S. Millennium Challenge Corporation: providing assistance only to those countries that can demonstrate progress in building strong private sectors, creating employment, and strengthening governance.

Australia, Ireland, the Netherlands, and Sweden have also completed assessments of their aid programs that call for improved evaluation, more local ownership, and better institutional capacity in governments. They found that successful projects involved local initiative, good governance, measured results, and the creation of local institutions for sustainability.

Other donors, particularly the World Bank, have attempted to measure programs for results such as poverty reduction. The Bank's evaluation unit found that its poverty reduction record remains problematic. In a 2006 evaluation of twenty-five Bank-assisted countries, only eleven were said to have reduced the incidence of poverty between the mid-1990s and early 2000s, with poverty either stagnating or increasing in the remaining fourteen countries. (Private sector organizations in the United States and other developed counties have also been actively engaged in projects bearing on development in low-income areas for many decades. With some notable exceptions, foundations, private and voluntary organizations, and corporations have not generally evaluated their projects for results at the impact level.)

---

*Local ownership [of aid-funded projects] increases the prospects of long-term success by involving local institutions.*

---

The U.S. Agency for International Development (USAID) has a long history of evaluation using primarily process and output measures. While some serious, impact-level evaluations have been conducted, the numbers have been low relative to total projects and money committed by USAID. Nor does information from these evaluations or others seem to be used to inform USAID design and implementation decisions. . . .

## Shared Characteristics of Successes

*Local Ownership and Initiative.* Successful programs and projects reflect actual needs of the recipient countries as expressed by local actors, rather than simply reflecting instructions of what projects and programs may be available for local recipients from USAID. Local ownership increases the prospects of long-term success by involving local institutions. Such partnerships can, indeed, lead to the continuation of institutional relationships between American and partner leaders long after the end of USAID funding. The Rotary Club campaign to eliminate polio succeeded because of the ownership and financial commitment of local Rotary Clubs throughout the developing world.

*Partnership.* Successful projects and programs demonstrate collaboration between American and developing-country institutions, especially private institutions. Indeed, such collaboration seems virtually essential for a sustained engagement that brings benefits valued by all. The U.S. government should always attempt to ensure partners are committed to a program before it makes an investment; as a general rule, the U.S. contribution should be the second or third dollar on the table, not the first. When everyone is committed to common priorities and has made an investment, then everyone will be accountable for the results. With mutual accountability comes sustainability. The Consultative Group for International Agriculture Research, which spawned the Green Revolution, was a partnership among governments, foundations, and the private agribusiness sector.

---

*Long after USAID's financial role has ended, U.S. foreign assistance can allow America's professionals and institutions to build relationships with their developing country counterparts on the basis of perceived professional self-interest.*

---

*Leverage.* The U.S. government can take advantage of the myriad new sources and techniques of global support for developing countries, including foundations, private voluntary organizations, corporations, universities, and remittances. USAID alliances with new American philanthropic activities overseas can help leverage resources that far exceed those contained in federal budgets. Such partnerships can recognize the priorities and expertise of philanthropic leaders and their institutions. Similar strategies can be used to link U.S. programs to emerging local business leadership in developing countries. Within this framework, USAID would become not a controlling taskmaster of U.S. development programs, but an aggregator or facilitator of effort, the creator of syndicates of resources targeted at self-reliance. While small in scope, USAID's Global Development Alliance has successfully leveraged government funds with contributions from private companies, foundations, charities, and universities. This type of partnership should constitute the business model for virtually all U.S. foreign assistance in the future. . . .

*Peer-to-Peer Approaches.* Long after USAID's financial role has ended, U.S. foreign assistance can allow America's professionals and institutions to build relationships with their developing country counterparts on the basis of perceived professional self-interest. Such opportunities are exemplified in USAID's Hospital Partnerships Program, through which U.S. physicians volunteered their time to work directly with physicians in Eastern Europe and the former Soviet Union. This peer-to-peer approach is patently superior to the contractor model that currently dominates USAID programming.

*Technology Adaptation and Adoption.* Some of the most widely acknowledged foreign assistance successes, such as the Green Revolution, have at their core the application of technology to improve the human condition. As the scientific and technological capacity of developing countries expands, so does the potential for technology partnerships in foreign assistance. Local ownership is also important in this context, as integration of technology such as bed nets and oral rehydration salts is vital to ensuring their effective use within the communities where they are introduced. Local foundations' growth and social entrepreneurship's successes in developing countries have shown how technology can work for poor people throughout the world.

*Self-Reliance.* The most important steps taken to improve the long-term success of developing nations will come from within those countries. In successful and self-sustaining projects, local leaders are the engines of change. Conversely, encouraging leadership and good policies may mean ending or reducing aid to a country. We must not be afraid to withdraw funds to ensure that assistance does not result in dependency in recipient countries. . . .

## A New Business Model

The pervasive lack of convincing evidence of significant macro-impact from past foreign aid efforts, the changing nature and capabilities of the developing world, and the emergence of new sources and approaches to resource transfers for development all point to a single conclusion: U.S. foreign assistance needs an entirely new business model.

> *Allocations of U.S. development aid should favor sustainable public-private partnerships in the host country.*

Sectoral and project earmarks, directions, and limitations in foreign aid legislation are a "design for failure" and should be removed, with the exception of those deemed essential to U.S. national security. U.S. foreign assistance programs should be able to respond fully and flexibly to demand-driven opportunities emerging within developing countries.

With the exception of expenditures deemed essential to U.S. national security, the United States should avoid distributing foreign aid without monetary or monetized resources coinvested in and by the recipient country itself. Such in-country organizations may include local affiliates of U.S. NGOs and corporations, indigenous foundations, local businesses, and public agencies. Allocations of U.S. development aid should favor sustainable public-private partnerships in the host country.

The main competition for U.S. foreign assistance dollars should not be among consultants but among ideas coming from the multiple actors now involved in foreign aid and philanthropy, particularly on the demand side of the equation in developing countries. Those who wish to attract U.S. resources should bring to USAID their best ideas and their own resource contributions from private sources, explaining their goals in terms of economic and social impact, local ownership, partnership with local institutions, and achievement of community self-reliance. USAID should operate more like a foundation (and less like a disbursement agency), articulating areas or problems of interest and inviting competition for new approaches. . . .

The new business model for foreign aid proposed here departs from the past in at least three important ways. First, it is based on flexibility. The programs pursued, the opportunities seized, the partners aligned, and the ways in which funding creates self-reliance are driven not by earmarked legislation, not by the capacities of contractors, not by the world of 1970, but by the nature of the problems and the presence of opportunities from the promises of a changing world.

Second, it reduces centralized control. USAID becomes not the taskmaster of U.S. development programs but an aggregator or facilitator of efforts and a creator of syndicates of resources targeted at self-reliance.

Third, it permits—indeed, even emphasizes—innovation. USAID would seek fresh faces, new approaches, new technologies, and new mechanisms for allocating its resources. It would seek out and link its activities to new streams of resources, looking for leverage for every dollar it dispenses—or, more hopefully, invests—and constantly searching for emerging cofinancing leaders. This business model transforms USAID from a passive funder of projects to an investor in innovation.

# 13

# Developing Nations Want Free Trade, Not Foreign Aid

*Njoroge Wachai*

*Njoroge Wachai is a Kenyan journalist who has worked for the Kenya-based* People Daily. *He has also worked as a correspondent for international news services, including the* Bulletin of the World Health Organization.

*Foreign aid, however well-intentioned, has too many conditions and obstacles to be an effective force in combating poverty in developing African nations. Aid money sinks these needy nations further into debt and encourages African governments to subsist on handouts. The solution to Africa's problems is trade, not aid. Africans need to get access to markets in order to better their industry and reinvest capital in the future of their countries.*

G8 [Group of 8 industrialized nations] Summits are fast becoming synonymous with Africa's miseries. It's almost predictable that at the top of the agenda of every G8 Summit is how Africa is dealing with the triumvirate issues of poverty, political instability and disease. In the 2005 G8 Summit in Gleneagles. Scotland, it was Darfur [a conflict-ridden part of the Sudan]. In this year's [2008's] Summit in Japan, it was a threat to impose sanctions on Zimbabwe for holding a fraudulent election and suppressing the opposition.

Actually, it has become fashionable, prior to and during these summits—forget what happens when they're concluded—for G8 leaders to pledge tens of billions of dollars to help Africa fight poverty. These are usually in the form of aid and debt cancellations.

During the Gleneagles Summit, G8 countries pledged, with much fanfare, to double aid to Africa by 2010. This was after a sustained and highly publicized international campaign by celebrity musician Paul David Hewson, a.k.a Bono, and music producer Bob Geldof's Debt AIDS Trade Africa (DATA), that rich countries extend their hands of "generosity" to Africans.

---

*It goes without saying that rich countries are lethargic about passing their money to Africa, because it doesn't make economic sense to do so.*

---

## Reluctant Donors, Needy Recipients

Some G8 leaders, I guess out of shame, did offer to forget and forgive debt to a select group of African countries. Thanks to them, some African countries' debt burden has been lessened. At least some progress has been made on this front. Countries such as Tanzania and Ghana have been redirecting funds that could have been spent servicing foreign debts to social programs, with some remarkable success.

But there has also been grumbling about the pledge to increase aid to Africa. The African Progress Panel 2008, which monitors fulfillment of G8 pledges, has a pugnacious report that asserts that, "the pledge to double assistance to Africa by 2010, made at the G8 Summit at Gleneagles in 2005, is not likely to be fulfilled." The report claims that out of the $25 billion in additional aid pledged to Africa in 2005, only $3 billion has been made available. Japan, Italy and France have been singled out for doing particularly little to fulfill their pledges.

This year's G8 Summit, which just concluded in Japan, has revisited the aid issue. The rhetoric is as it was in 2005. G8 leaders have announced a $60 billion package to help Africa fight HIV/AIDS, malaria and tuberculosis. Place your bets on whether this latest pledge will be fulfilled or will remain just a pledge. Which belies the question: Why do African countries keep pushing for aid that rich countries are reluctant and unwilling to give? Isn't there an alternative?

## Aid Will Not Bring Prosperity to Africa

Africa's fixation with foreign aid is amazing. Foreign aid isn't freebie stuff. It goes without saying that rich countries are lethargic about passing their money to Africa, because it doesn't make economic sense to do so. Those of us who live in these rich countries can't understand this notion of rich countries "giving" money to Africa.

The Americans, Britons, Canadians or French don't give money away for free. Were this the case, those of us Africans who live here would be very prosperous. We'd be receiving subsidized housing, education and medical care. There'd be affirmative action laws in these countries to help qualified Africans land high-paying jobs so that they might, in turn, invest back home in agriculture, health care and education, the darling sectors of the donor community. Immigration laws would be as friendly toward Africans as they are toward Cubans, Liberians, Vietnamese and, yes, Europeans.

> *The idea that foreign aid will move Africa out of poverty is a fairy tale.*

After all, these are the same Africans whom G8 countries are dying to help. They're the same folks who come from the continent where men, women and children go without food; where millions of children die of preventable diseases such as malaria, tuberculosis, and diarrhea; and where children learn under trees because there's no money to build classrooms.

African leaders, out of their foolishness, believe wrongly that rich countries are philanthropic entities flush with cash to dole out to poor countries. That's why they, or their representatives, are always in Western capitals with begging bowls.

The idea that foreign aid will move Africa out of poverty is a fairy tale. Look at the policy governing food aid in the U.S., for example. Congress demands that all food aid be procured from American farmers, shipped by American-registered ships, and distributed by U.S.-based relief organizations. What this means is that virtually all the money the U.S. earmarks for food aid remains within the U.S. Relief organizations and the shipping industry have been lobbying hard to oppose any change in the status quo. In the meantime, dependency syndrome continues to take its toll on African countries that find themselves unable to produce enough food for their populations.

## Increase Trade, Not Aid

It's high time African countries realized that foreign aid comes with too many strings attached to be considered a good weapon to fight poverty. Donor countries disburse aid thinking first and foremost of their own bottom lines; after all, they have taxpayers to be accountable to. For instance, we've had cases where donor countries give out money for infrastructure development in African countries, but demand that those projects be undertaken by their own construction companies at a cost specified by them. These countries also dispatch their own astronomically well-paid "technical assistance experts" to oversee these projects. They end up gobbling the biggest portion of "donated" funds, with the remaining morsels going to the corrupt high and mighty in the countries they serve. No wonder that Africa is still right where it was fifty years ago, when the concept of foreign aid emerged.

Trade, not aid, is what Africa needs. Rather than make promises of more aid for Africa, rich countries should increase the volume of trade with Africa.

# 14

# The "Trade, Not Aid" Strategy Has Not Helped Developing Nations

*Justin Frewen*

*Justin Frewen is a consultant with the United Nations. He is a doctoral candidate in political science at the University of Galway in Ireland.*

*The belief that trade, not foreign aid, will lead developing nations toward prosperity is questionable. Though open trade policies may help, so far they have been misused and misapplied. While the industrialized global North has made free trade a part of their assistance philosophy, these economic powerhouses are more often than not simply finding new markets for their goods and resisting the importation of products from the developing South. For example, industrialized nations have retained tariff barriers on imported goods yet require that developing nations drop their protections. As a result, developing nations are flooded with cheap goods with which domestic manufacturers cannot compete. If free trade is not made equitable, then developing nations will not benefit from opening their markets.*

Despite pledges on the part of donor countries in 1970 to spend 0.7 percent of GNP [gross national product] on official development assistance (ODA), this target is still proving elusive 40 years later. Many would argue that ODA is not the best way to tackle poverty and its attendant ills, and that the solution is increased global trading: By ensuring the inclusion of all countries, particularly poorer nations, in the worldwide trading structure and networks, poverty could be eliminated.

At the same time, other analysts would hold that free trade has frequently been used to cloak efforts by wealthier nations to further strengthen their economic dominance as well as to obstruct the development efforts of poorer countries.

For the majority of economists, the critical factor in tackling poverty is economic growth. The solution to achieving this required growth, they argue, is the increased promotion of free trade on a global basis. For these commentators, the failure to adequately integrate developing countries into the world market is the real obstacle to the elimination of poverty.

## Criticizing the "Lift All Boats" Philosophy

Mike Moore, ex-head of the World Trade Organization (WTO) and a strong free trade supporter, stated in August 2008, "Seven years ago, we introduced at Doha [a round of trade talks that took place in Doha, Qatar] what was to be a 'development round.' All trade rounds are. President [John F.] Kennedy, who introduced the Tokyo round, famously said, 'This will lift all boats and help developing countries like Japan.' Case made, I would have thought."

*The current free trade model has been widely criticized as preventing developing countries from introducing economic reforms suitable to their own growth and poverty-reduction needs.*

However, there are many who have questioned the link between trade liberalization and economic growth. According to the development theorist, Richard Peet, "The past two decades have seen a rapid opening up to trade in developing countries … [and] trade volumes in developing countries have grown faster than the world average. … This massive increase in exports has not added significantly to developing countries' income."

Moreover, the current free trade model has been widely criticized as preventing developing countries from introducing economic reforms suitable to their own growth and poverty-reduction needs. By imposing a "one size fits all" approach, states in the global South have seen their range of development policy measures seriously curtailed.

Whereas nations such as Britain and the United States utilized tariffs and other economic policies to nurture industrialization, these options have been greatly reduced. The Cambridge economist Ha-Joon Chang claims that powerful states, despite having employed interventionist economic policies to facilitate their own growth, now prevent developing states from adopting similar measures.

## Trade Double Standards

It is in this respect that the WTO [World Trade Organization], the foremost international trading body, has been widely criticised. The WTO was established with the principal objective of liberalizing and promoting free trade to foster global economic growth and development. However, its real contribution to increased trade is debatable. As American economist Andrew Rose, a free-trade advocate, noted, "Membership in the GATT [General Agreement on Tariffs and Trade]/WTO is not associated with enhanced trade, once standard factors have been taken into account. To be more precise, countries acceding or belonging to the GATT/WTO do not have significantly different trade patterns than non-members."

Moreover, many in the South accuse the WTO of double standards. Rather than being a neutral forum, they believe the

WTO acts as a lever for the North to increase its economic influence. Although states in the North constantly demand market liberalization, they are often slow to implement it themselves. A particular flashpoint in this respect has been the North's protection of its agricultural sector. The Trade-Related Aspect of Intellectual Property Agreement has also proved highly controversial. It established a global 20-year protection period with monopoly trading rights for patent holders, which appears to fly in the face of the WTO's free-trade ethos.

*There is a widespread and growing conviction in the South that the North is using the concept of free trade both as a means to pry open their domestic markets while ensuring their global economic hegemony remains unthreatened.*

Perhaps most damning of all is the fact that the majority of trade agreements, both inside and outside the WTO, have relatively little to do with the promotion of free trade. These agreements tend to be predominantly concerned with the imposition of rules, including conditions on how services can be delivered or the appropriate manner to regulate foreign investors. They appear more concerned with creating a homogenous global marketplace, where the South is at a disadvantage.

At the same time, little attention is paid to levelling the international trading playing field and ensuring the South a greater share in global wealth. There is a widespread and growing conviction in the South that the North is using the concept of free trade both as a means to pry open their domestic markets while ensuring their global economic hegemony remains unthreatened. The real problem would appear to be not the South's lack of integration into the world market but rather the terms under which it has been integrated.

## Creating Winners and Losers

Rather than helping the South reduce poverty, the current international free-trade structure is actually aggravating it. Already in a weakened position, the South is now also deprived of many of the economic policies it needs to tackle them.

Although, free trade supporters contend that the opening up of global trade has paved the way for dynamic economic growth that has, in turn, led to a reduction in global poverty levels, this decline in poverty has been predominantly in just two countries, China and India. The reality has been quite different in the majority of other countries in the South. Furthermore, research has shown that, in fact, economic growth in a country such as India has not appreciated significantly subsequent to its adoption of a liberalized trading system.

The only real progression would appear to have been the escalating growth in inequality between the winners and the losers in the global marketplace. This inequality has socially devastating consequences with increased levels of violence, higher rates of social exclusion and marginalization, and reduced life expectancy. It would therefore appear unwise to rely on the ability of our current free-trade system, through some sleight of its invisible hand, to alleviate the evils of poverty, hunger and inequality.

# 15

# Amateur Philanthropists Benefit Foreign Aid Policy and Practice

*Josh Weinstein*

*Josh Weinstein has served with several advocacy programs that help the world's poor. He resides in Nairobi, Kenya, working as a consultant to Bridge International Academies, a chain of low-fee private schools serving the urban poor. He also runs the Develop Economies blog.*

*Professional foreign aid institutions have not always succeeded in addressing the needs of the world's poor. More often, amateur aid organizers have helped target needs and found funding for projects that make a difference in the lives of the poor. Not every amateur succeeds, but trial and error has proved a better method of finding aid solutions than sticking to many traditional models. That experience of trying, failing, and learning from mistakes has given many amateurs the vital expertise to serve needy communities more effectively than large, professional aid groups.*

In my experience, development professionals tend to be a jaded and cynical bunch, but also eternally optimistic, well-meaning, and principled. In one post, a blogger who writes "Good Intentions are Not Enough" (another blog I read and respect) explains what it means to be an "aid professional." Here are a few:

Josh Weinstein, "Why DIY Foreign Aid Amateurs Are Necessary," *Develop Economies*, October 26, 2011. http://developeconomies.com. Copyright © 2011 by Josh Weinstein. All rights reserved. Reproduced by permission.

- First and foremost—Do No Harm—whether what we do is right or wrong, we are doing it to the people that can least afford for us to fail.

- There is a need for fresh perspectives and a variety of ideas and approaches. However this must be tempered with knowledge of the factors that led to success and failures in the past so the same mistakes are not constantly repeated.

- Stick around long enough for projects to have a chance to fail. Then try to stop them from failing and learn from your mistakes.

---

*How can experts bring a fresh perspective if they all draw from the same pool of knowledge?*

---

While I agree with these principles, I don't think the status quo promotes them. Yet "Good Intentions" is right—we need to learn from mistakes. Some of my good friends in Ghana worked for Engineers Without Borders [EWB] Canada. One was a mechatronics engineer, another a geoscientist (by training, not profession). The amateurs at EWB Canada even created a website called "Admitting Failure" and held a conference called FailFaire, which is cited by professional development workers as a step in the right direction. To fault "amateurs" for their mistakes, while saying experts should learn from theirs is a bit hypocritical in my opinion.

## Amateur Aid Warriors Often Do Better Work Than Government Programs

Regarding the second point—how can experts bring a fresh perspective if they all draw from the same pool of knowledge? Successful projects bring expertise and best practices from many different fields and apply them to development. This is how you bring fresh ideas.

And, most importantly, regarding "do no harm," Overlapping mandates and a lack of coordination between aid agencies operating within the same industries and regions can not only undermine private sector development by providing a glut of services at subsidized costs, but also fail to optimize resources. Of course, do no harm. But don't assume that amateurs will do more harm than "professionals".

In my personal experience, the most innovative and effective organizations and companies are the ones founded by development amateurs with a professional background in other fields—the self-taught warriors who bring their insight and skills from other industries to bear on the social sector.

---

*[Amateurs] may not always succeed, but, if history is a guide, applications of traditional development theory haven't produced overwhelming results either.*

---

My intention isn't to say that everyone with a Masters Degree in international development and a resume overflowing with public sector and development experience is wrong about everything. Clearly, that experience is valuable in understanding context and knowing what has worked and not worked in the past. It is particularly relevant in the policy sphere—designing programs like Bolsa Familia [a Brazilian social welfare program] or advising governments on legislation and policy.

Rather, I want them to recognize the critical role amateurs play in this work. They bring new ideas, enthusiasm, optimism, and interdisciplinary skills drawn from diverse backgrounds in manufacturing, retail, technology, and other industries. They may not always succeed, but, if history is a guide, applications of traditional development theory haven't produced overwhelming results either.

## Failures of Status Quo Thinking

The second and more important point is that this "leave it to the experts" mentality is far more destructive in the long-run than the trial-and-error nature of DIY foreign aid. Some critics feel that failed ventures like PlayPumps [an organization that sought to bring clean water to sub-Saharan Africa] draw money away from other projects and ventures that might work. This, to me, is a recipe for the status quo—an approach to poverty alleviation and economic development marked by a lack of innovation, fresh ideas, and competition for funding dollars.

---

*Among the amateurs . . . the failure rate may be high, but successes can be far greater.*

---

Among the amateurs, the failure rate may be high, but successes can be far greater. PlayPumps may have been a failure, but what about Kiva? Kiva—an online peer-to-peer lending organization that uses the Internet to connect lenders with borrowers around the world—might the most successful and effective non-profit in modern history. It has more than one million users and has distributed over $250 million in loans to borrowers in 216 countries. . . More importantly, it is fully financially sustainable—something that is paramount to the founders, Matt Flannery, Jessica Jackley, and Premal Shah, who cut their teeth at technology companies and leading business schools.

## Everyone Can Make a Difference

Out here in Kenya, I see former lawyers, software programmers, investment bankers, management consultants, journalists, engineers, college students, product managers, teachers, physicians, and tech entrepreneurs starting and working for successful nonprofits and social enterprises. Few of them are "experts"—in fact, nearly all of them come from the private sector in their previous lives.

> *My advice to anyone who is thinking about quitting their job and taking up the cause of making the world a better place: do it.*

These people are what development economist Bill Easterly calls "searchers." Searchers, in contrast to planners, seek to find what works, but do not assume that they have all of the answers. In "Planners vs. Searchers in African Agriculture Aid," Easterly describes the differences between the two groups:

> Planners announce good intentions but don't motivate anyone to carry them out; Searchers find things that work and get some reward. Planners raise expectations but take no responsibility for meeting them; Searchers find out what is in demand. Planners apply global blueprints; Searchers adapt to local conditions. Planners at the top lack knowledge of the bottom; Searchers find out what the reality is at the bottom. Planners never hear whether the planned got what it needed; Searchers find out if the customer is satisfied.
>
> It is thus impossible to design rewards for success or failure for Planners, because we will never know which agents' interventions failed or succeeded. A Searcher can "own" an intervention, and get rewarded if it succeeds and not rewarded if it fails. So Searchers have better incentives and better results.

The attributes Easterly describes are often associated with successful practices outside of the development sector. This is why individuals with different skills and experiences can bring a fresh perspective to an industry dominated by planners.

So here is my advice to anyone who is thinking about quitting their job and taking up the cause of making the world a better place: do it. Don't hire a professional. Don't even try to become a professional. Should you read a book or two about what works and think about how you can maximize your impact without being detrimental? Definitely. But don't be afraid to challenge the status quo. Ignore the "professionals" telling you to leave this work to the experts. Try something. If you fail, learn from it. If you succeed, share it, and help others to scale. Don't be deterred by people telling you that you don't have the experience. Just go out and do it.

Over the past two years, I have seen innovative and creative minds building great things.

# 16

# Amateur Philanthropists Often Harm Foreign Aid Policy and Practice

*Dave Algoso*

*Dave Algoso is a graduate student of international development at New York University. He writes about aid issues at his blog* Find What Works.

*The do-it-yourself philosophy has been spread across the media and has influenced several social and political arenas. In the case of providing aid to the world's disadvantaged, there is a new belief that amateurs can solve the problems that professional aid organizations cannot. This is a dangerous trend. Although the intention of "doing good" for others should be respected, amateurs simply lack the experience in handling the complexities of foreign aid. When their projects fail, no one is held accountable. They may even unintentionally do harm simply because they misjudge the needs or customs of the community they wish to help. Foreign aid is best left to experts who have the connections and training to avoid such pitfalls.*

Many globally minded, can-do Americans these days have come to believe that the world's major problems have solutions, and that these solutions are within reach. This feeling often leads to frustration: Why doesn't someone just *do* something about these problems? Are the NGOs [nongovernmental organizations] and foreign aid agencies lazy, incompetent, or both? Why can't we end poverty?

Last weekend [in late October 2010], the *New York Times Magazine* ran a cover story about people who have taken matters into their own hands. The piece, Nicholas Kristof's "D.I.Y. Foreign Aid Revolution: The rise of the fix-the-world-on-your-own generation" offered several aren't-they-inspiring stories about Americans who have run off to save poor people in developing countries from whatever afflicts them. A woman from Oregon begins fundraising for community work in eastern Congo, and later shifts her attentions to conflict minerals. A recent high school graduate from New Jersey uses her babysitting money to start an orphanage and school in rural Nepal. You get the idea.

---

*Spend a little time in any community in the world, and you'll see people from that community finding ways to improve it—not outsiders.*

---

The stories sound lovely. I admit to feeling a little warm and fuzzy inside reading them. After all, this is what drives me to do development work: to make the world just a little better. (I study international development at New York University.) We all want to tell ourselves the story about fighting through hardship—each of these women made personal sacrifices for their work—to make the world a better place.

## Local Leaders Have the Best Solutions

Unfortunately, such stories don't reflect reality. Spend a little time in any community in the world, and you'll see people from that community finding ways to improve it—not outsiders. Working in eastern Uganda last summer, I found well-organized community groups who weren't waiting for any outsider's help. I worked with an NGO that conducted business and financial skills education in rural villages, and our best trainers were Ugandans from those very villages.

Yet these sort of people—local community members help-ing their neighbors and themselves—are absent from Kristof's stories. Instead, he gives the reader an American heroine (his stories are mostly about women) who comes to save the day. Local individuals exist as needy targets of the protagonist's be-nevolence. If they act on their own behalf or the behalf of their community, it's only after the American has prompted them to do so. Developing country governments and domestic civil society are barely mentioned. Saundra Schimmelpfennig, who blogs at Good Intentions are Not Enough, has dubbed this the "Whites in Shining Armor" storyline: Americans and other outsiders are uniquely positioned to bring change to a community, as if we are saviors come to deliver them from poverty.

> Being an outsider supporting development in a commu-nity raises difficult questions with both moral and strate-gic dimensions.

Such implicit arrogance aside, a more fundamental prob-lem is that Kristof's narratives make development seem *simple*. In his stories, the hero sees a problem and fixes it. Women are suffering from war and rape in Congo? Raise some money, build some homes, and regulate conflict minerals. Lack of af-fordable sanitary pads keeps women from work and girls out of school? Develop a cheaper pad. Orphaned children in Ne-pal? Build an orphanage. He even implies that the established foreign aid organizations "look the other way" when it comes to these problems. How could they miss such obvious oppor-tunities for improving lives?

## Making Sure Aid Serves the Needs of Recipients

What Kristof misses is that even seemingly obvious solutions are more complicated than they appear. Development means change, and change is always complicated—and often political. . . . Being an outsider supporting development in a community raises difficult questions with both moral and strategic dimensions.

Here's one critical question: How can we ensure that the work actually serves the best interests of the beneficiaries, when the funding comes from the other side of the globe? A community's needs may be too complex for foreign staff and volunteers to understand, and too nuanced for a fundraising pitch. Outsiders in the community may see homeless children and relay the need for an orphanage to donors. With a few pictures to tug at heartstrings, the money starts flowing in. However, those children might be better off living with members of their extended families, and the same resources that built the orphanage would be better spent providing support to make this happen. Unfortunately, that work requires a deeper understanding of the community and a more complicated fundraising message.

*The development industry is by no means perfect, but it has made progress and learned valuable lessons. The lessons are often ignored by newcomers, and the same mistakes are made over and over again.*

Another question that's often overlooked: What impact do outside money and volunteers have on the local economy, political structures, and culture? Adding a wealthy outside investor can skew incentives in unexpected ways. Local businesses lose market opportunities when NGOs give donated goods away, for example. Similarly, local officials face less pressure to provide public services or cultivate a sustainable tax base when donors fund schools, health care facilities, and infrastructure. And since it is outsiders—not the government—providing those services, citizens have no means to hold them accountable for quality. Political and economic changes can also have unintended cultural impacts. For example, an agricultural project dividing communal land into private farming plots can weaken social ties. Even programs with intended cultural impacts have unpredictable repercussions in all spheres.

## The Development Industry Has the Experience That Amateurs Lack

The world of aid has spent the last 50 years grappling with these questions. The development industry is by no means perfect, but it has made progress and learned valuable lessons. The lessons are often ignored by newcomers, and the same mistakes are made over and over again. Kristof nods toward this fact while breezing past it. He focuses on the passion and indignation of his heroines while downplaying their technical abilities.

I have nothing against the individuals described in Kristof's article. The concerns I expressed above apply to all development organizations—they just happen to be especially relevant to small and new ones. Admittedly, every organization starts small and new. Muhammad Yunus spent decades developing the Grameen Bank model before winning the Nobel Prize. Paul Farmer delivered health services to rural Haitian communities for years before Partners in Health became a world-renowned organization. There have been books written about entrepreneurs like Yunus and Farmer, and the years they have spent understanding the communities they work in, refining their work, and building their organizations.

But other initiatives fail, and sometimes they draw massive support away from worthier projects before that happens. A recent high-profile example is the PlayPump, a merry-go-round that would let village children pump clean water as they play. An initiative to install PlayPumps across Africa received millions of dollars from the U.S. government and other donors—until the high cost of the pumps, their potential to break down, and their basic inefficiency led to a drop in support. PlayPump's backers were lured by the mirage of a quick technical fix to a seemingly simple problem. But providing clean water was harder than it looked.

---

*A project that misunderstands the community or mismanages that crucial relationship can undermine local leaders, ultimately doing harm to the very people it was meant to help.*

---

Yet Kristof's headline is: Do it yourself. Bring the same attitude you would have toward re-painting the living room or installing a new faucet. After all, how hard can it be? The developing world is like your buddy's garage. Why not just pop in, figure things out, and start hammering away?

## Amateurs May Do Unintentional Harm

But in this field, amateurs don't just hurt themselves. A project that misunderstands the community or mismanages that crucial relationship can undermine local leaders, ultimately doing harm to the very people it was meant to help. There are also opportunity costs when funding could have been used better. Every dollar spent on PlayPumps or an unnecessary orphanage could be spent on other, better interventions in the same communities. My advice is to hire a professional. And if you want to do this work yourself, become a professional.

Despite all my complaints, I think Kristof's article does some good if it convinces more people to pursue international development as a career. We all start as amateurs. The difference is whether we seek to learn more or assume that we can just start doing something, muddling through as we go. The "D I Y foreign aid" concept might spur a few people to launch ill-advised ventures that eat up scarce resources and get in the way of better efforts, but it might also convince a few others to read a couple books, go to graduate school, get jobs with professional aid organizations, and spend their whole careers making a real impact.

# Organizations to Contact

*The editors have compiled the following list of organizations concerned with the issues debated in this book. The descriptions are derived from materials provided by the organizations. All have publications or information available for interested readers. The list was compiled on the date of publication of the present volume; the information provided here may change. Be aware that many organizations take several weeks or longer to respond to inquiries, so allow as much time as possible.*

**American Enterprise Institute (AEI)**
1150 17th St. NW, Washington, DC   20036
(202) 862-5800 • fax: (202) 862-7177
website: www.aei.org

The American Enterprise Institute (AEI) is a nonpartisan, nonprofit organization that has sought since its founding in 1943 to advance liberty, individual opportunity, and free enterprise in the United States through research, debate, and publication. Video of AEI scholars and conferences on the topic of foreign aid such as "Empty Wallets at Home, Crises Abroad" and "The Road to Better Aid: An Emerging Bipartisan Consensus," as well as articles such as "Focusing Foreign Aid on Entrepreneurial Development," can be viewed on the AEI website. *The American* is the monthly magazine published by the organization.

**Brookings Institution**
1775 Massachusetts Ave. NW, Washington, DC   20036
(202) 797-6000
website: www.brookings.edu

The Brookings Institution is a public policy organization that utilizes its original research to craft policy suggestions that improve American democracy, advance economic and social opportunity, enhance national security, and connect individuals, organizations, and governments around the world. One central topic to these goals is the US provision of foreign aid to developing countries. Brookings has hosted numerous conferences to foster the discussion of this issue and many reports, including "From Aid to Global Development Cooperation" and "Capacity for Change: Reforming US Assistance Efforts in Poor and Fragile Countries," as well as opinion based pieces on this topic, such as "Congress and Foreign Aid" and "Better Than Expected US Support for Global Development," can be read on the institution's website.

## Cato Institute

1000 Massachusetts Ave. NW, Washington, DC  20001
(202) 842-0200 • fax: (202) 842-3490
website: www.cato.org

The Cato Institute is a libertarian think tank dedicated to promoting ideals such as individual liberty, free markets, and peace through its research, commentary, and policy suggestions. Generally, the organization and its scholars have opposed the provision of US foreign aid as a tool to promote development in countries worldwide. Studies such as "The False Promise of Gleneagles: Misguided Priorities at the Heart of the New Push for African Development," as well as articles and commentary such as "What Can Aid Do?" and "US Foreign Aid Hinders More Than It Helps" expand upon this view. The Cato website provides access to these articles and numerous others on this topic.

## Center for American Progress (CAP)

1333 H St. NW, 10th Floor, Washington, DC  20005
(202) 682-1611 • fax: (202) 682-1867
website: www.americanprogress.org

The Center for American Progress (CAP) is a progressive public policy institute that works to make the lives of all Americans better by promoting policy suggestions that counter conservative policy, pressing the media to address pertinent issues, and framing these issues for the national debate. While the organization supports the use of foreign aid as a tool for development, it emphasizes the importance of carefully selecting the recipients to ensure the most effective use of the funds. Reports such as "US Foreign Aid Reform Meets the Tea Party," and an interactive map allowing users to explore how and where US aid is spent, can be accessed on the CAP website. Additional opinion pieces and research are also provided on the website.

## Center for Global Development (CGD)
1800 Massachusetts Ave. NW, Third Floor
Washington, DC   20036
(202) 416-4000 • fax: (202) 416-4050
website: www.cgdev.org

The Center for Global Development (CGD) is an independent, nonpartisan think tank dedicated to promoting development in an effort to eradicate poverty and inequality worldwide. The organization conducts research in specific areas such as aid effectiveness, education, globalization, health, migration, and trade to examine where governments as well as non-governmental organizations should place their focus to foster the broadest development. The commitment to development index on the Center's website offers visitors an interactive map to explore the ways in which developed countries provide aid to developing countries. Reports on the effectiveness of foreign aid and its relationship with other development goals including trade, migration, and investment can be read online as well.

## Congressional Budget Office (CBO)
Ford House Office Building, 4th Floor, Second and D Sts. SW
Washington, DC   20515
(202) 226-2602
e-mail: communications@cbo.gov
website: www.cbo.gov

The Congressional Budget Office (CBO) is the US government office that provides objective, nonpartisan information to the US congress on budgetary matters. The office examines all programs implemented by the government using funds from the federal budget. The CBO has examined the provision of US foreign aid and its effectiveness over the years, and its website provides access to reports and testimony on this issue.

### Future of Freedom Foundation (FFF)

11350 Random Hills Rd., Suite 800, Fairfax, VA   22030
(703) 934-6101 • fax: (703) 352-8678
e-mail: fff@fff.org
website: www.fff.org

The Future of Freedom Foundation (FFF) is a libertarian organization seeking to promote ideals such as individual liberty, free markets, personal property, and limited government through its publications, conferences and meetings, and media appearances. With regard to foreign aid, the organization has taken a hard-line stance against the practice and has called for an end to all US foreign aid. Articles such as "Time to End All Foreign Aid Entirely," "But Foreign Aid Is Bribery! And Blackmail, Extortion, and Theft Too!" and "Condolences Yes, Assistance No" present this view and can be read on the FFF website. The organization's monthly publication *Freedom Daily* can also be read online.

### Heritage Foundation

214 Massachusetts Ave. NE, Washington, DC   20002
(202) 546-4400
e-mail: info@heritage.org
website: www.heritage.org

A research and education institute, the Heritage Foundation has been working since 1973 to promote conservative values such as free market economics, minimal government, individualism, traditional American values, and a strong national defense. In accordance with these beliefs, the organization's stance on foreign aid has emphasized the importance of American assistance that focuses on improving developing countries' governments and economic policies to foster an environment favorable for continued development. Reports such as "The US Should Link Foreign Aid and UN General Assembly Voting" and "US Foreign Aid: Not All Development Assistance Is Equal" offer a refined explanation of these views and can be read online.

## Organization for Economic Co-operation and Development (OECD)

2001 L St. NW, Suite 650, Washington, DC   20036
(202) 785-6323 • fax: (202) 785-0350
e-mail: washington.contact@oecd.org
website: www.oecd.org

The Organization for Economic Co-operation and Development (OECD) has been fostering cooperation between member governments for 50 years in an effort to advance economic and social-well being for individuals around the world. The organization works directly with governments to create a more nuanced understanding of the drivers of change and to create implementable strategies to make this change a reality. One area of focus is development, and within this area, OECD has focused reports and conferences on determining the effectiveness of aid in development. Reports such as "Better Aid: Managing Development Resources" and transcripts of speeches like that of the OECD Secretary General, "How to Maximize Impact on Development," can be accessed on the organization's website.

## Oxfam America

226 Causeway St., 5<sup>th</sup> Floor, Boston, MA   02114
(800) 776-9326
e-mail: info@oxfamamerica.org
website: www.oxfamamerica.org

Oxfam America works at an international level to find ways to end poverty, hunger, and social injustice globally. One means of doing this is through foreign aid. Oxfam generally supports the giving of US foreign aid as a means of increasing development and improving stability in developing countries. Field reports from individual countries receiving US aid can be read on the Oxfam website, along with more general articles and video clips detailing the reasons why this monetary assistance is necessary.

## United Nations (UN)
140 East 45$^{th}$ St., New York, NY   10017
(212) 415-4000
website: www.un.org

The United Nations (UN) is a global organization that was created following World War II to foster international cooperation between member countries. Over the ensuing decades, the UN's mission has expanded and specialized to focus on multiple areas, including peace and security, development, human rights, humanitarian affairs, and international law. The United Nations Development Program focuses specifically on the ways in which developing countries can best be assisted to become more economically and politically stable. This office's website provides detailed information about the Millennium Development Goals used to help measure countries' progress and the aid they should be given. Additionally, articles on the interplay between foreign aid and assistance with other issues such as the environment, trade, and technology can be found on this site.

## US Agency for International Development (USAID)
Information Center, Ronald Reagan Building
Washington, DC   20523-1000
(202) 712-4812 • fax: (202) 216-3524
website: www.usaid.gov

Created in 1961, the US Agency for International Development (USAID) is the US government agency charged with determining which developing countries receive foreign aid and distributing federal government funds accordingly. This monetary assistance is given with the goal of advancing American interests while helping these countries to make the lives of their citizens better through increased economic prosperity, democracy, health, food security, education, environmentalism, conflict resolution, and human rights. Information about specific agency programs within these areas and regionally based programs can be found on the USAID website.

# Bibliography

## Books

| | |
|---|---|
| Terry F. Buss with Adam Gardner | *Haiti in the Balance: Why Foreign Aid Has Failed and What We Can Do About It.* Washington, DC: Brookings Institution, 2008. |
| Robert Calderisi | *The Trouble with Africa: Why Foreign Aid Isn't Working.* New York: Palgrave Macmillan, 2006. |
| Paul Collier | *The Bottom Billion: Why the Poorest Countries Are Failing and What Can Be Done About It.* New York: Oxford University Press, 2007. |
| William Easterly, ed. | *Reinventing Foreign Aid.* Cambridge, MA: MIT Press, 2008. |
| William Easterly | *The White Man's Burden: Why the West's Efforts to Aid the Rest Have Done So Much Ill and So Little Good.* New York: Oxford University Press, 2006. |
| Carol Lancaster | *Foreign Aid: Diplomacy, Development, Domestic Politics.* Chicago: University of Chicago Press, 2007. |
| Dambisa Moyo | *Dead Aid: Why Aid Is Not Working and How There Is a Better Way for Africa.* New York: Farrar, Straus and Giroux, 2009. |

| Louis A. Picard and Terry Buss | *A Fragile Balance: Re-examining the History of Foreign Aid, Security and Diplomacy.* Sterling, VA: Kumarian, 2009. |
| Linda Polman | *The Crisis Caravan: What's Wrong with Humanitarian Aid?* New York: Metropolitan, 2010. |
| Roger Riddell | *Does Foreign Aid Really Work?* New York: Oxford University Press, 2007. |
| Jeffrey D. Sachs | *The End of Poverty: Economic Possibilities for Our Time.* New York: Penguin, 2005. |
| A. Maurits van der Veen | *Ideas, Interests and Foreign Aid.* New York: Cambridge University Press, 2011. |

## Periodicals and Internet Sources

| Elliott Abrams | "Conservative Foreign Aid," *National Review*, November 28, 2011. |
| Katherine J. Almquist | "U.S. Foreign Assistance to Africa: Securing America's Investment for Lasting Development," *Journal of International Affairs*, Spring/Summer 2009. |
| Jean-Paul Azam | "Foreign Aid Versus Military Intervention in the War on Terror," *Journal of Conflict Resolution*, April 2010. |
| Ben Barber | "Fixing Foreign Aid," *Foreign Service Journal*, October 2011. |

| | |
|---|---|
| *Economist* | "The Big Push Back," December 3, 2011. |
| Arthur A. Goldsmith | "No Country Left Behind? Performance Standards and Accountability in US Foreign Assistance," *Development Policy Review*, January 2011 Supplement. |
| Richard N. Haass | "The Restoration Doctrine," *American Interest*, January/February 2012. |
| William P. Hoar | "Foreign Handouts: More Harm Than Good," *New American*, February 15, 2010. |
| Richard Ilorah | "Trade, Aid and National Development in Africa," *Development Southern Africa*, March 2008. |
| Kristian Kjøllesdal and Anne Welle-Strand | "Foreign Aid Strategies: China Taking Over?" *Asian Social Science*, October 2010. |
| Daniel Yuichi Kono and Gabriella R. Montinola | "Does Foreign Aid Support Autocrats, Democrats, or Both?" *Journal of Politics*, April 2009. |
| Richard G. Lugar | "Foreign Assistance: Strengthen the 'Third Pillar' of National Security," *Human Rights*, Winter 2008. |
| Thandika Mkandawire | "Aid, Accountability, and Democracy in Africa," *Social Research*, Winter 2010. |

| | |
|---|---|
| *New Internationalist* | "Should Foreign Investment Replace Aid for Africa?" September 2011. |
| Mathew O'Sullivan | "Restructuring U.S. Foreign Assistance in The Wake of the Arab Spring," *Washington Report on Middle East Affairs*, September/October 2011. |
| Gustav Ranis | "Giving up on Foreign Aid?" *Cato Journal*, Winter 2011. |
| David B. Skarbek and Peter T. Leeson | "What Aid Can't Do: Reply to Ranis," *Cato Journal*, Winter 2011. |
| Rebecca Stubbs | "The Millennium Challenge Account: Influencing Governance in Developing Countries through Performance-Based Foreign Aid," *Vanderbilt Journal of Transnational Law*, March 2009. |
| Matthew S. Winters | "Choosing a Target," *World Politics*, July 2010. |
| Joseph Wright | "How Foreign Aid Can Foster Democratization in Authoritarian Regimes," *American Journal of Political Science*, July 2009. |

# Index

## A

Abugre, Charles, 47–51
Accountability
  amateur philanthropy, 102,
    105, 107
  America should aid nations
    which show progress against
    goals, 70–80
  America should aid nations
    whose governments demon-
    strate, 65–69
  donor nations, 25, 68
  failures, with aid, 29
  Millennium Challenge Corpo-
    ration model success, 40–41,
    44–45, 78
Accra Agenda for Action (2008),
  71
Adelman, Carol C., 81–90
Afghanistan
  aid totals, 32
  US foreign aid and national
    security, 16, 33
  US foreign aid led to 9/11,
    61–62
Africa
  Canadian aid totals, 85
  clean water initiatives, 104,
    111–112
  development potential, 13–14
  disease and aid programs,
    82–83, 93–94
  economic growth, 51
  French aid history, 25
  skepticism about aid, 13, 14,
    47–51, 66, 92–93
  US aid history, 7

US aid needs, 36
US aid totals, 32, 34, 53, 66
wants trade, not aid, 91–95
Aga Khan Foundation, 83–84
Agricultural production
  Africa, 51
  intellectual property issues, 99
  key to development, 12, 13,
    51, 87, 88
  Millennium Challenge Corpo-
    ration programs, 45–46
"Aid model," 23–24, 29–30, 46, 70
Aid package size
  African aid, 48–49
  bias for large amounts, 25–26
  macro-to-local aid format,
    84–87
Aid totals, US. *See* United States
  aid appropriations
AIDS programs, 37, 40, 42, 50–51,
  76, 93
al-Qaida, 17, 62
Algeria, 56
Algoso, Dave, 107–113
Amateur philanthropy
  benefits foreign aid policy and
    practice, 101–106
  often harms foreign aid policy
    and practice, 107–113
American values, 19–20, 21, 37–
  38, 57
  *See also* Democracy, spreading
Anti-retroviral drugs, 42
Anti-terrorism programs, 59, 61
Applegarth, Paul, 8
Arab Spring revolutions, 2011, 41,
  55–56, 57–58, 60, 61, 63